HUSH LADIES MEN ARE TALKING

BY
C. J. BIG

Published by
Janet's Link Ink
www.hushladiesmenaretalking.com

Printing in the U.S.A.
First printing, 1st Edition
Cover Photograph © 2008 and
Design by:
Janet's Link Ink

LIBRARY OF CONGRESS
CATALOGING-IN-PUBLICATION
BIG, C.J.
HUSH LADIES
MEN ARE TALKING

ISBN 978-0-9817544-1-3

For ordering information go to:
www.hushladiesmenaretalking.com

Special Thanks
To My
LORD AND SAVIOR
JESUS CHRIST
FAMILY AND FRIENDS!!!

DEDICATION

I want you to know this book was written for the sole purpose of enlightening, educating and empowering.
My Gift to You!!!

HUSH LADIES
MEN ARE TALKING

BY: C. J. BIG

THE AGE OLD DILEMMA

Since the beginning of time when God created man and woman, there have always been issues between them. I guess that's why God took a rib from man. I believe God was sending a message to man that woman would forever be a thorn in his side.

The very first account of a woman not listening to her man was of course the apple incident. Adam said to Eve, now baby, don't forget, do not eat off that tree. God said don't do it. One day Eve went off just kickin it and ran into one of her so, called friends. Eve's friend said; *come on Eve, let's eat one of the apples off that tree. No I can't. My man told me not to. He said God forbids it. Girl you a fool! Your man doesn't know what he's talking about. He just doesn't want you to be as powerful as him. Girl don't be no fool, you better eat one of those apples. I'm trying to help you out! Your man wants to keep you ignorant so he can tell you what to do. I'm telling you girl, your man has already eaten off that tree. Don't be a fool girl! Go ahead and eat an apple.* She bit the apple, and well we know the rest of the story. She just couldn't listen to her man.

What about Lot's wife? He said to her, *God's about to get mid evil on this whole city. God is sparing my family because I have been shown favor in his sight. All we have to do is keep walking and don't look back. So baby, I'm telling you, keep it moving and don't look back. What did Lot's wife do? She stopped, turned around and looked.* She's still, to this day, a pillar of salt. Once again, all she had to do was listen to her man.

Believe it or not, the first account of baby, momma drama is also in the Bible? That's right. This is when Sarah insisted her husband Abraham, have sex with her Egyptian maid servant Hagar to get her pregnant. All because Sarah thought she could not get pregnant. Abraham said; *no baby, that won't be necessary. God already promised us he was going to bless your body and give us a son.* Sarah said, *listen Abraham, I'm way past my child bearing years. Now do like I tell you, go sleep with Hagar and get her pregnant.* It was against Abraham's better judgment but he did it anyway. He just wanted to satisfy his wife. Hagar got pregnant by Abraham and gave birth to a son and his name was Ishmael. Soon after, God did what he said and blessed Sarah's body. She too became pregnant by Abraham. Sarah gave birth to a son also, and he was named Isaac. Shortly after Isaac was born, Sarah went to Abraham and said, *Hagar and her son Ishmael got to go! Neither Ishmael, nor his mother is getting any parts of inheritance from this kingdom.* Abraham did not like it but he sent Hagar and Ishmael away. Now if that ain't baby, momma, drama, I don't know what is. All Sarah had to do was listen to her man. There are numerous accounts of women not listening throughout the Bible. Now of course, I'm not quoting word for word from the Bible, but please read it for yourself. Believe me it's all there.

My mother used to tell me "*there's nothing new under the sun. If you want answers, go to the Bible. God won't mislead you*". But, did I listen? Dad would say; "*just ask me. I'm gone tell it like it is*".
In my younger years I preferred going to Dad, he seemed more real to me. Many years later, combined with a multitude of failed relationships, I learned Dad, definitely was no authority. Thank God, for the bible.

One day a good friend of mine said, *I'm so tired of women and their bullshit! I just don't understand. How a female can lay down with a man, have sex with him, give him a blow job but won't listen to his advice? The only message a woman is giving to a man is, you can give me a sexually transmitted disease like syphilis, aids, or even a baby, but she won't take his advice to heart.*
This has got to be the most messed up way of thinking. What can we do to change this? I feel lost. I don't want to be in a relationship where a woman does not respect what I have

to say. I could clearly see the seriousness in his eyes. I wanted to tell him what my mother taught me. *Go to the Bible.* However, everyone is not as biblically inclined as I am. So I turned to the three wise men, Robert, Rick and Chico.

I wanted to talk to these three men because they are known for mentoring young men. They agreed to set up a forum for the men to discuss their concerns regarding women. Two weeks later Mr. Chico called and said; *we'll meet at Robert's crib. This will be the best place because he has a big house, with lots of privacy. Robert, Rick and myself will supply all the ribs and steaks, but the younger men must do all the barbecuing. We will also supply beer and cognac, but anything else you must bring yourself. No women, no children, and no one under the age twenty five.* I began contacting some of my friends and much to my surprise many men were eager to participate.

The day of the "Big Meeting". I was impressed. The back yard was beautiful to say the least. Every one that was invited had shown up. Most of the younger men were already standing around the huge barbecue pit, engulfed in a cloud of smoke, cueing meat, laughing, talking and turning up beers. Just the smell made me instantly hungry. The few men that were not around the grill was chillin in the lounge chairs on the deck. The Elders: Rick, Robert, and Chico, were relaxing in their tilt back chairs, drinking cognac, and beer, laughing and talking, with some old school Temptations playing in the back ground...

Chico, this is nice. Never in my many years of life have I ever been so overwhelmed! Come on Rick, you trying to tell me after thirty years in the medical field this is thrilling? I would think by now nothing could excite you! Chico, this is different. Just look around. Three generations of men are here. Yeah Rick, this is a large group. Chico and Rick remember in the past we were always a part of the younger age group at these events?

Now, we're the *elders'.* Yeah Robert, unfortunately, nowadays there are so few older men who takes the time to help a young brother. I know what you mean Rick. However, we're here and our theme for today's *meeting* is "women". So, Rick and Robert do both of you think this open forum is going to help these young men get a better understanding of the women? Hell Yeah! Chico, it's got to, better yet, let me put it this way, it can't hurt. Robert, I think you're right.

You know Chico, I've found most advice these young men ask for is regarding problems with females. I know what you mean Rick. The toughest situations I've had to deal with in mentoring young men all involved women. Well, isn't that with all men? Nothing and no one can twist up a man's mind like a woman. You should know Chico; you've had enough of them. Well Robert, which one of us hasn't had his fair share of dilemma's when it comes to women? You're right about that Chico.

That's why I believe this discussion is so important. Sometimes men need to speak open and honestly about what they think and feel concerning women. Also, with the diverse age group from 25 to 70 we should be able to cover every situation that arises. Who knows, maybe, next year we can make it much larger. Well Rick, before we start thinking about next year let's get through this one. Okay Chico.

Hey Tony! Check those ribs! I think it's time to turn them over! We don't want burnt meat. Look Mr. Robert, I got this! All ya'll need to do is just sit over there and let the young men handle this grill. You hear that Chico? Yeah Robert. I tell you, these "new school" boys think they know everything. Chico, when I was in my twenties and thirties I thought I knew everything too. An old school brother couldn't tell me nothing. Yeah, Robert, I was living for the weekend. Hell yeah Rick! Whooo! I remember some of those weekends. I say some cause a few times I was too drunk to remember what the hell I did or who I did it with. I know that's real Chico! I used to have so many women I couldn't keep up with their names. Chico you couldn't keep up with their face either. I remember when you hit on the same woman you had just had sex with the night before. Remember? You know Chico, the one you was too drunk to remember? Then you got up the next day and left before she woke up because you didn't want to give her your phone number. She really cussed you out. Yeah Robert, I remember. I was embarrassed as hell. I know Chico you were embarrassed but me and Rick laughed our ass off. That is still funny.

Y'all over here talking about women, or should I say reminiscing about when you had women? Aw, here we go, another know it all young blood. I don't profess to know it all but I was with two hunnies last night that made me prove my manhood for about three and a half hours. You call that proving your manhood Kenney? Hell yeah! You think it wasn't Mr. Robert? How old are you Kenneth? Thirty one, never married, and no baby momma's; Oh, well that explains it.

Hell, at thirty one, no children, and unmarried, you're right; the only things you have to do to prove your manhood is work a little and fuck a lot. Mr. Chico, was that supposed to be some kind of a dig? Mr. Rick, it ain't that funny. Alright, Kenneth don't get uptight. We're just having a little fun. Yeah man but at my expense. Tell me the joke so I can laugh too. Man you came over here cracking on us. We're just giving it back. Kenneth, look, I know you think it's proving your man hood when you conquer several women through sexual gratification. At your age, I used to think the same thing. But, as you get older and run into that right woman, then you'll understand what we're laughing about.

Man Mr. Robert don't you think I want to settle down? I really do. But the females today are different then when you guys were young. What do you mean? Alright old school, let me teach you. Come on young brother enlighten us. Oh, here we go again with the jokes. Go ahead Kenneth, we're listening. On the real. When I got grown that was my number one directive, find the right girl, get married, have children and by my calculations we should be working on our second son. Well, what happened? Mr. Rick, I got out there and women taught me something totally different. You know what I mean? Naw, but we're trying. Go ahead break it down, so even us old men can understand. No seriously, Mr. Robert, if you want me to tell it like it is, then no disrespect intended but, I'm gone have to keep it real. Okay Kenneth, but you know the two words we don't use. I got you Mr. Rick. Now go ahead. Okay, peep this;

When you're out there dating you can't tell if you got a …

...Trick or Treat (Kenneth)

What did you say Kenneth? Mr. Robert, I said it exactly like I mean it. About three months ago I met this fine, sexy, classy, woman at the premier of one of my plays. I introduced myself to her even though I knew she was already aware that I was the producer. I saw her as she came in and watched in anticipation for the right moment to approach her. Eventually I got the chance to talk to her and we exchanged numbers.

I was so excited about going out with this girl that I made sure every date was well planned. Over a period of six weeks I took her on fourteen dates. We walked along the Lake Front, dinner downtown, plays, movies, and had flowers constantly delivered to her job. All the classy things a man like me would do. She was the perfect lady, but I could not seem to impress her. No matter what we did at the end of the evening she still appeared just as distant as if it were our first meeting. It was driving me crazy. But, of course it was also exciting to chase this woman. I had to have her.

At the beginning of the seventh week I got so desperate I even went to some of my guy's and asked them to give me some ideas on how to get this girls undivided attention. My boys and I came up with the ultimate date. So the next time we got together I took her to the Signature Room in the Hancock building for dinner and a carriage ride touring downtown. Then, I paid the carriage driver to sit and wait while we took a walk around the Buckingham Fountain. After all of this when I walked her to the door and reached to kiss her, she made it short but sweet; this was her usual way of saying thanks and have a good night.

Man, right then and there, I got so frustrated I lost all parts of cool. I just put it out there. I said what is it going to take to be with you? Man y'all ain't gone believe what this woman told me! Come on Kenneth what did she say? Mr. Chico, she said, *"some weed and a bottle of Martel."* What! You bullshittin! No I ain't! I swear Mr. Chico! That's what she said. Man I was so mad! I started to tell her to go to hell! Well did you? Hell naw! I thought about all the money and time I had spent on this girl. I had to get something for my efforts. Shit man, I made a phone call to fill her order and sho-nuf she filled mine. Hey Kenneth, was it worth it? Hell naw! I was too mad. I kept thinking about how I believed she was the right one. Only to realize once again I had the *trick*, instead of the *treat*.

Man I get so tired of these ungrateful females. I'm the type of man that automatically indulges females in the manner in which they should be treated. This was the way I was raised. But instead of being honored for being a respectable brother, I'm instantly given labels such as soft, gay, lame, boring, and let's not leave off the fatal title of a trick. I'm not any of these degrading names, I am a Man.

Most of the females today are unappreciative, undignified, and mentally constricted. However, I realize their misguided lack of judgment is not totally their fault. I believe it's a direct result of their elders releasing them into adulthood unskilled, untrained and uninformed in the ways of how a real woman should be respected. Although this is not entirely their fault, unfortunately, it is their burden.

Whoa! Kenneth, young man, slow down, you seem a little bitter. Mr. Chico, I am! Hey, Kenneth, if you had one opportunity to tell women something that you feel will help them to have a better relationship with their man what would you tell them? Mr. Chico, that's easy. I would tell them; for those women who have grown tired of assassinating their own womanhood there is hope. It's called, change! There are a number of things she can do and the main fix starts with modifying her thoughts on what a woman is and what it means to be a good woman to a good man. This understanding alone will help her to decide if she's up to the challenge of becoming a true woman or if she'd rather maintain her present status as an emotionally reckless, maltreated individual.

I believe too many females are unaccustomed to the traditional ways of a lady, leaving this species of women vastly becoming extinct. Women should know it is customary that a door be opened for her. Her chair should be pulled out. It is normal that she be called by her birth given name instead of B#*@&, baby girl, yo baby, momma, etc… These names should be degrading to a ladies soul. But, instead it has become the norm. The mistreatment that a large number of females allow themselves to endure is awful to say the least.

So many women are making the conscious decision to assassinate the tenderness of the lady that dwells within them. This is a major part of what separates a woman from a man. I'm a genuine man! I will not become the least bit content with a female who wants to be anything less than a lady. To lower my standards in a woman say's one thing, I'm willing to reduce myself as a man. This is a thought I will not entertain. I need a woman that requires the reverence of a queen.

The truth is, a lot of the women today have lowered their standards to rock bottom. All a brother has to do is come over and kick it at the females crib. You might need to bring a drink and something to smoke. But, some just want you to show up.

Well Kenneth! What exactly are you looking for in a woman? Mr. Robert, the same thing every man wants in a woman.

Now, Kenneth, you can't say every man because what's important to you, as far as good traits in a woman, may be exactly what another man can't stand. Okay Kenneth, you're thirty one year's young right and I'm at least twenty years older than you. Daaammnn, Mr. Robert, you that old? Don't go there Kenneth. My bad, go ahead. Do you think I need the same things in a woman you require? Naw, not the sex part anyway. One mo dig and I'm gone show you what twenty additional years of experience can put on you. Alright, Alright, I ain't gone call you old no more. Now go ahead Kenneth and finish telling us what your ideal woman is before I forget I'm your mentor.

Alright, on the real. I am a man who has all five senses intact. My ideal woman has got to be prepared to feed all five. In my sight I need to see our house clean and my woman dressed like a lady. This is such a turn on. I'd like to walk in my door after a difficult day of work to see a beautiful, well dressed woman. This reassures me that the shit I put up with all day is worth it. Shit Kenneth, the only thing I want to see my woman wearing when I get home from a hard day's work is silence, some shut the fuck up, some be, on, quiet Tony man that was funny as hell! Now you put on that same outfit you want her to wear and let me finish. Alright, alright, go ahead Kenneth, man. Well thank you Tony.

I have two ears that I use to listen to anything she wants to tell me. Now if she takes this opportunity to fill my ears with positive reinforcement, I guarantee listening to her will become one of my greatest joys. I also have a keen sense of smell. When I walk into our home and the aroma of food is slowly simmering on the stove and the smell greets me before I can even open the door, this makes me weak at the knees. My taste buds get to watering and I can hardly wait for the food to hit my tongue. But, this does not top the fresh scent of my woman. This makes something else wait in anticipation and dance. Right then and there if I was angry or upset about anything when I came in the door, trust me I will put it on the back burner of my mind.

Last but far from least, I need to touch her. I want to stroke every inch of her soft, gentle, skin, making sure I satisfy every portion of her body. Trust me, I will happily show my appreciation by any means necessary. We must feel the need to feed one another mind, body, and soul. To me these are the cornerstones of creating a great relationship. I'm not saying it's easy but, these are the things that make it ever so worth it. I intensely crave this blend in a woman.

I've had ladies ask me, *"Why should I go through all of this and the man leaves or cheats on me anyway"*? Then I answered their question with another question. Is being less of a woman supposed to serve as an invisible, protective shield that limits some of the continuous indignities you may suffer within a bad relationship? No relationship is without its challenges. However, some relationships are worthy of your dedicated, efforts. On the other hand, some men should have never gotten past the first phone conversation. Honestly, if a lady is in a relationship and not being respected as a lady, she should run. The sacrifice is too great. The one thing she should *never* be willing to compromise is being treasured as a woman. I guarantee preserving the lady within her will definitely minimize the ill-treatment she will undergo. But, that's if being treated like a queen is truly what she desires.

The truth is, I'm finding more and more women non-supportive of a good man. They say he's too demanding. So instead of going through the necessary challenges it takes to be with the right man, she lowers her standards in what she expects from a man. But, she then forgets to change the actual expectations of the outcome in the relationship. She cannot bond with a man who is satisfied with making $10.00 an hour when her goals, hopes, wishes and desires are to own a multimillion dollar corporation in five years. It's not going to happen. Before you know it, a woman will start complaining about all he is not, and how she's not happy within their relationship. Women need to seriously understand, when they decide to change their ideology of a man they also need to get a whole new set of dreams. Because if they think for one minute, less of a man can fulfill the life she's dreamed of with a financially successful man, trust me her thinking process is definitely delusional. I can even put it simpler; wrong man, subtract dreams, equals depression. Believe it!!!

So Kenneth what would you tell a woman if she wanted to pursue a man like you?

A genuine man will not become less inferior to satisfy her lack of womanhood. We will however, have plenty of sex with her. But, she'll never become the wife.

When a man like me tells a woman what he needs and she decides not to provide it, this does not mean he's not going to get it. This simply means he's not going to get it from her. You cannot put a man on a shelf and take him down when you think it's time for you to give him some undivided attention. Trust me this is just in your imagination. It may appear he's been there waiting all along but in reality he wasn't on your illusionary shelf, he was with someone else.

Women, who can't cook, don't like to clean, and believe being sexually submissive is for white women, don't waste my time, you need not apply. This statement is non-negotiable.

Demand more of what you desire from a

man then don't back off. For example: if every time he goes out with his friends and don't come in until two or three in the morning and this pisses you off each time. By all means leave him. Stick to your guns. You must make a man a believer. He will respect you for it.

Don't do certain things to get him then stop once you're in a relationship. Once you start it you must not stop. It will always be a part of the core of your relationship.

Treat the whole man not just one part. I guarantee he will surely be your *"Doctor Feel Good"* in return with pleasure.

Love truly is something that time and adversities cannot take away so make sure when you give yourself to someone it's for love not for the love of your plan. Because if you are not in love it will not last!!!

I'm working on being the next billionaire. I need a woman who's up to the challenge of working right beside me.

Man Kenneth, I know what you mean. I learned the difference between being...

...THE KING AND I (Mike)

I remember being single, I thought I was the man. Women would come to my crib; they'd sit on my big ass leather couch, relax on my big ass easy chair, watch my big ass screen television, shower and dry off with my big ass thick towels. Then they would lay on my big ass king size bed. Everything was big, brown or black and screamed masculinity. Damn, Robert, it sounds like Mike is describing your house. Go to hell Chico. Go ahead Mike. Don't pay Chico any attention. As I was saying, every time anyone would come in my house they would always say "you can tell this is a single man's house". Even my mother would visit and make the statement, "there's no doubt about it this is a single man's house".

One night I was chillin at the crib, watching the game on my big screen television, when the door bell rang. My dad and a couple of his friends had stopped by. I felt like I was the man. Here I am a man amongst men in my kingdom. My father's friend said *"Damn!" "I can tell you're a single man."* With great pride I said "yeah, I'm the king of this castle." My dad laughed and said *"you might have a castle but you damn sho ain't no king."* What! Dad you've got to be slippin! I'm the king up in here! I pay all the bills, and everything in here is mine. *"Like I said, you got a castle but you ain't a King." "Without a Queen all you are, is exactly what you keep saying, and I."* Everybody laughed but me. It was at that exact moment I realized I was only a single man. No matter how much big ass furniture I brought or how much I paid for it, I was only a single man; single, alone, just one; the loneliest number in the world. Trust me, I'm a teacher. I can do the math.

One of the most profound statements ever made is, "*there's no place like home*". A man's home is where he goes to find respect, peace, concentration, happiness and solitude. This is where he is the king.

I didn't say Ambassador, Senator, Doctor, Lawyer, etc… for these titles depict working for someone else. I said King. A king does not work for the good of himself but for the good of everyone in his kingdom (household). The best thing is, he can never be referred to as an I. And, the only true boss he has is God. But there is one catch to becoming a King. YOU MUST HAVE A QUEEN! Without a woman sitting beside you, the only thing you'll always be is a plain, old, I. A single entity, a mere shadow of the man he could be. Finding the right woman to help fulfill your dreams is the most important goal you must achieve.

I don't envy single men today. Finding a queen within this present social order is virtually impossible. It's like trying to find a sober woman in a crack house. This is because far too often in today's society many women have been displaced. Oh, here you go professor. Whatever Tony, man, it's the truth. It's really hard for a man to find a queen because women are forced into roles that carry them far from their natural origin of being a lady. Their obligations consist of being the father, because you have too many baby daddies and not enough fathers. She has to be the disciplinarian in order to dilute some of the chaos that could arrive from the lack of supervision while she's at work making the money to take care of her family. Not to mention she's the coach, mentor, referee, entertainer, maid, short order cook, liaison, and the list goes on and on. Because of all these responsibilities, being a woman to a man becomes all too problematic.

As a teacher, I work predominately with women. They talk about dating as though it's something you have to steal. Like the police is going to arrest them for simply loving their man. It's that real. One lady I work with say's "occasionally, she sneaks a night away from her busy schedule to capture a few stolen moments of passion with her man." *Sneak* and *steal* should not be the terminology used when it comes to spending time with your man. I know for me, seeing a woman under those circumstances would do absolutely nothing for my sexual appetite. The bad part about it is women don't realize they themselves are the only ones that can change this.

This predicament of displacement goes deeper than multitasking. Man, another lady at work said, "She feels like a she/he." She also said, *it's like society has handed her a set of balls and told her to wear them until she finds a man she can trust with her balls.* Damn! Yeah, but, wait Tony, check this out, it gets deeper. She continued on to say; when she does get a night out with her man, temporarily she hands over her balls to him. Then she can allow herself to be vulnerable at that moment and just be his woman. She said *you have no idea how good it feels to let go of those balls.* Then morning comes and suddenly she's unable to trust her needs or his wants. So she snatches back her balls and returns to her dual life as a she/he. Now that's deep.

This is why it's so hard to find a queen. Some of these females got it so twisted. Why in the hell would a woman even want to pretend to have a set of imaginary testicles? Half the time they don't know what to do with a vagina.

Until she said that, I never really understood the magnitude of how some women viewed their whole situation. I asked her what is the solution. She said, *for men to return to their natural foundation of a man*. Yeah, but I had to ask her, ain't you the one who's walking around with imaginary balls? Women need to get their minds right first. They need to quit walking around here thinking they got balls. They don't! That's the bottom line. Therefore, it is up to women who think like that to transform back into the original queens God intended them to be.

This is why so many men are choosing to live alone. Men's options as far as dating appear to be narrowed down to two selections. First he can choose to date a younger woman who has not developed the big balls syndrome. However, he'll be draped with the immature drama that comes from her lack of experience. On the other hand to deal with an older woman means going through the changes of convincing her to get rid of the imaginary testicles that she thinks is bigger than his. I've heard women say several times, and I quote *"I got my own car, crib, career and cash." I can do whatever a man can and better".* Every time I hear a woman say this, the only thing I have to say to her is: does having your own, make him less of a man? To tell the truth, I'd rather be single, than a miserable, castrated, remnant of a man living with a woman who's got the balls. God made me a man fully equipped with a set of balls. I definitely don't need a female to hand me my man hood. Every day I thank God, for blessing me with my Queen. Our relationship is just like many couples, it has its challenges. But I'd rather go through the disputes and work on solving our differences than to face the alternative.

So Mike what would be the best advice you could pass on to the next man and woman in their endeavors of dating? Yeah, sum it up for us professor. Don't hate Tony.

Well Mr. Rick, My only suggestions would be…

Know your role. I'm a man who has to be the king in his home. Now it's not easy being the leader. But, I'm not a follower. Not in our home. I work hard, pay the bills, help raise the children, and maintain a structured, comfortable, life for my family. But, not alone; my queen is right there beside me keeping it all together and loving me even when it's not going so well.

It's okay for a woman to be tough while she's away from her man. Her man's presence, please, please, please, be gentle. If she insists on being tough it will only dilute the true essence of love that can exist.

Ladies, if a man wants you to be his Queen, make sure he is ready to be your king. Do not subject yourself to undue pressures from a man who does not fit the criteria. He should at the least be putting forth great effort.

You know Mike, I've listened to you and Kenneth and for the most part I agree with what you're both saying. But, I'm a single man like Kenneth. And the women out here are simply not ready for a serious brother. What do you mean Dave?

Mike, man when women come into my job I feel they're looking at me like I'm an ice cold glass of water on a one hundred and fifteen degree day. Man, you know what I'm saying, they're thirsty. Y'all can quit laughing. This Shit ain't funny. Man I get so tired of going through the process of looking for the right one. I don't even believe there is a right one. Dave man you shouldn't feel that way. Mr. Rick, no disrespect intended, but, fuck that! From my experience so far what I've learned, is most women are not ready for a serious relationship. I'm not even sure they know what a relationship entails.

If I could tell women what I really feel I'd say…

…Females Are To Easy To Sleep With And Too Damn Hard To Please (Dave)

Damn, man, no you didn't go there! Yes I did. You know its true Kenneth. A woman knows when she sleeps with a man too soon; the only thing she can expect is more sex. Don't y'all sit here and act surprised! What's left; a long standing relationship? I don't think so! Personally, I feel if it was easy for me to have sex with her it won't be hard for the next guy either. I'll drop her. But, if the sex was off the chain, I will keep her as a dip.

Why y'all gone sit here and act like I'm the only one who feels this way? I'm not a shallow man. When I first started out dating I was strictly looking for the right woman. Like Kenneth said, I went all the way out for my dates. Each and every woman I decided to take out was because I thought she was going to be my Princess or Queen as Mike said. Man that shit didn't happen. I couldn't make money fast enough. These dates were killing my pockets. Hell, I did all the things my Mother had taught me when dealing with a young lady. The problem was I didn't know the difference between a young lady and a gold diggin, date junkie. Date junkie? Yeah Mr. Rick, a date junkie is a female who goes out on as many dates as she can, and spend as much of his cash as possible. Breaking a brothers pockets off for plain old bragging rights. Damn that's cold. Yeah, you telling me.

In the beginning like I said, my intention was to find the right woman and get married. But, ladies taught me different. Each and every lady I've dated taught me how to treat her. When I ask a lady out on a date, I give her the option of choosing where we should go? If she say's dinner and a movie, that's what we do. She chooses the movie and the restaurant. After our date, I'll ask if she'd like to go back to my place for drinks and conversation. If she accepts my offer, comes home with me and we have sex, she has taught me her expectations are low, and the sex is easy. From here on out she will forever be known as an easy, cheap, sleep. I'll never treat her any different.

On the other hand if I take a lady out and she insists I take her home, I'll walk her to the door, attempt to become physical, but, if my advances are declined, she has just taught me I must try harder. She is now a challenge to me. We will definitely have a second date. But, nine times out of ten as soon as I drop her off, I'll call a cheap, easy, sleep and pick her up on my way home to cap my night off with hot sex. However, while we're getting busy, I'll be imagining that the woman I'm having sex with is the one I just dropped off. You know the one that didn't sleep with me. The sex will be off the chain. We'll reach a climax or two, then exhaustedly I'll turn over and with a smile, think about how nice it's going to be when I get to see the woman that turned me down.

Dave, why would you go and sleep with someone else? It's simple Mr. Robert. I would be so stimulated by the night's events I would want to get off; Nothing more, nothing less. That's it, that's all. It's not rocket science. I'm simply answering the call of physical desire. For all I know, after I dropped her off, she may have received some sexual healing herself. But, that's not my concern at that time.

If ladies want a man to take her serious, the man must invest time, energy, effort and money in her. When a man has taken her out several times, let's say about seven or eight dates, this is spending time, energy, effort and money. Now he feels he has a vested interest in her. After all those dates, it's imperative he receive the reward of intimacy. If he doesn't, he'll feel like a trick.

Also, after several dates he not only lust for her sexually he's had time to learn some intricate details about her and she has had the opportunity to get to know him better. If he's still around after several dates and appears to be just as interested, it's obvious he's ready to take it to the next level. Once they engage in sexual intimacy and it's just as good or better than they both imagined, you can bet he's ready to be in a committed relationship. The truth of the matter is he will definitely want her to become exclusive to him. Believe me; once a man feels he has a vested interest in a woman, he doesn't want another man to reap benefits from his investment.

When a woman takes the time to learn a man's favorite foods and cooks for him, *before they have sex*, this say's, you're worth it. When a man learns her favorite flower and has them delivered to her at work, *before they have sex*, this say's, you're worth it. When a movie she wants to see comes out and he makes sure he takes her to see it on opening night, *before they have sex*, this say's you're worth it. When she knows he loves watching Monday night football and she doesn't disturb him, *before they have sex,* that says he's worth it. When the love making begins she will be sealing an agreement not trying to seduce him into one.

The only other item I want to cover is self-esteem. When a man tells a woman how great he is and how privileged she is to be with him, this may be true. But, she should try to remember this does not lessen her as a woman. When a man makes statements such as; "No man will ever love you the way I do." Or another one is; "No man will ever treat you better than me." Let's not leave off the famous line of; "I can get any woman out there but, I choose to be with you. All those other guys want is sex." This is his way of slaughtering her self esteem. Killing her self esteem is a sure way of getting her to remain true to him. I don't say this with great pride; it's just the simple truth. I've been guilty of this crime in the past myself.

So Dave, sum it up for us. What do you need these sistas to understand? Speak like you're talking directly to the women.

As men, it is sometimes our own inabilities that are the true object of our need to lower a woman as a person. It's a control tactic to break down your confidence. However, there is a remedy to dilute his efforts of trying to lower your self esteem. It's simple. When he finishes giving you his list of how lucky you are to be with him, quickly turn to him and remind him of how spectacular you are and it is equally a privilege for him to be with you. Attempting to shatter someone's self esteem works both ways. He will soon stop using those statements on you.

Trust and believe in God, yourself, then your man. Keep things in this order and you will never entrust your self esteem in the hands of any man.

Stop dropping it like its hot, maybe then you won't have to keep picking up your heart like its cold. Shutting down your lower half and opening up your mind will save you a lot of emotional grief as well as

physical wear and tear.
Value yourself as a woman in your own right. Your own right means: there will never be anyone like you. Whatever you do, only you can do it that way because God made us all individuals.

There is a simple fact most women miss altogether. When a man asks you out he's already interested. Take this opportunity to get to know him; thereby, giving him the chance to get to know you. This part of the relationship is called the nurturing stage. It is during this time that respect for one another and knowledge of each other develops. Don't Rush This Process!

Men want to be in a committed relationship just as much or more than women. Keeping sex out of the equation in the beginning will enhance the chances of a serious relationship.

Last but not least, DO NOT OVER LOOK WHAT YOU TRULY FEEL! If your heart is saying something is wrong, please listen, it probably is!

Man Dave, when you talk about a woman with self esteem problems, you've opened a whole new set of issues with a woman. Don't get me wrong, I'm not saying that men don't have esteem problems but damn a woman won't let it go. I dealt with a female who gave me a valuable lesson that I'll never forget.

Man listen, let me tell you her…

...Body Was Tight But Her Mind Wasn't Right

(Charles)

I'm a man who is extremely busy with the business of life. Most of the time, I work six days a week. I'm a single father, working hard on my job and making a vigorous attempt at getting my own company to go global. When I don't talk to my woman it's always one of several variables; business, my children, urgent family matters or household emergencies. It's not that I haven't been thinking about her. It's just I'm trying to continue to be the great man she fell in love with.

While I'm working hard, being motivated by my thoughts of her, occasionally, I'll daydream of how great it's going to feel when I get with my woman. Of course I'm thinking she's on the same page. Hell naw! Without my knowledge I've quickly fallen victim to some crazy women's decision making process who belongs to the *five step program.* Five step program? Yeah, Mr. Chico. The five step program. Here's what happens when a female is a member of the five step program. Check this out. This is similar to the twelve steps A.A. program, except, this is held by her girlfriends. Man Charles you're crazy. I'm for real. I've figured it out. We all know in the beginning when you first meet a woman you're excited, she's excited, you answer all her calls and make time to see her even though it's putting you behind in handling your functions. Every thing's going great. Eventually you come to your senses and realize you have to get back to handling your business. But, it's okay. Because you've spent enough time, energy and effort with her to be secure in the fact she knows you're hers and she's mine. So you fall back into your normal routine, you ain't worried because you know yo shit is tight. You get back to work. Business as usual.

As soon as one day goes by and you don't

answer yo dam cell phone, a weak, insecure woman instantly reverts to the five step program. *Step 1*: the *WHAT IF, SYNDROME.* This is when she has not talked to you for a day or so and before you know it she has made the conscious decision to anticipate every worst case scenario possible. It usually goes something like this: ***What if*** *he's seeing someone else?* ***What if*** *he's really not that interested in me anymore?* ***What if*** *he's mad about something I said or did? What if something has happened to him?* After going through a host of negative bullshit thoughts, finally she comes up with the ultimate, ***WHAT IF*** *he's dead*?

Because of her lack of self confidence she has gave way to every pessimistic thought geared toward the total destruction of our relationship. She has even gone so far as to envision me dead.

After the *WHAT IF SYNDROME* has been played out, it's time for *Step 2.* of the program: Call Your Closest Dearest

Girlfriend. This I call the GIRL, NO HE DIDN'T, condition. This conversation go as follows: *This man has ignored my calls for the last two days.* ***Girl, no he didn't.*** *I mean, how low can you be? The last time we were together it was a night of hot passionate sex and he said it was just me and him.* ***Girl, no he didn't.*** *Now this man has not returned one of my phone calls.* ***Girl, no he didn't.*** *I'm so hurt. He had me thinking it was just me and him and he pulls some shit like this.* ***Girl, no he didn't.***

Now while she's talking to her girlfriend, let's keep in mind she's playing with her own feelings. She goes from feeling sorry for herself; to mad as hell! Then the dialogue transforms into Step 3 of the program: The, *I KNOW THAT'S REAL, DISORDER.* This chatter starts off like this: *I can't wait till I hear from this no good, lying, cheating, dog!* ***I know that's real!*** *I'm gone let him know I ain't gone deal with garbage like this!* ***I know that's real!*** *This is the first and last time he's gone pull this shit on me!* ***I know that's real!***

Now that everything she has said is real because her girlfriend has co-signed on her points of anger it's time for Step 4 of the program: The *THAT'S WHAT YOU SHOULD DO DISEASE.* This is how it goes: *I know, when he does decide to call I won't answer!* ***That's what you should do.*** *Let him see how it feels when he can't get in touch with me!* ***That's what you should do***. *Then when I do talk to him I'll act like everything's cool.* ***That's what you should do***.

Now that I've been declared guilty by her and the jury that is not, of my peers, it's time for my sentence. Step 5: The ***IT'S TIME TO LET THAT GO,*** virus. But, this exchange in banter goes a little bit different. *Girl,* ***IT'S TIME TO LET THAT GO***. *You're right. You need to come on and go out with us Friday night and get your party on.* **THAT'S WHAT I SHOULD DO.** *Yeah girl, you know it's time to move on when they start pulling shit like this.* ***I KNOW THAT'S REAL.*** *Hurriedly she gets off the phone because she* *feels so bad and all she can think is,* ***WHAT IF*** it's really over.

Its official, the conversation has gone full circle and the poison has been injected. It's too late to turn back now. The five step curriculum of venom is flowing through her veins. Even she can't stop the infection from spreading. Now she's off the phone, sitting there with the remnants of what used to be a good relationship. She realizes her feeling of dread has escalated to intense sadness. Her alliance now, is to the program. She's in a no win situation. When her man does contact her she must carry out her directives. If she doesn't she will feel like a fool. You cannot undo the damage of the five step program.

Then to add insult to injury when you talk to her she will actually have the nerve to say; "*well if you had just returned my calls!*" As if that is some strong point to stand on. If she was so concerned about our relationship why wouldn't she allow herself to have positive thoughts like: *I know he loves me and he's probably extremely busy.* Women need to try this thought on for size:

If women would just realize subjecting their relationship to their girlfriends is the fastest way to mutilate his and her bond. I don't want a woman that believes discussing our issues with the sistas, is an option. The other thing is how can she say this is the man for her, then turn around and give him every negative thought she can think of without cause or provocation. A woman without strong self confidence will always subject her man to the negativity she's drummed up in her own mind.

I was once in a relationship with exactly the type of female I'm talking about. This woman had me so twisted. She had me believing shit I knew wasn't true. Mr. Robert, She had me second guessing my own sanity. For no good reason at all, this woman would lose her damn mind!

Where you been Charles? Who were you with Charles? Why did you have to go over there Charles? When did you leave work Charles? Man I couldn't do nothin without twenty questions. Shit, my life was one big ass explanation. But, don't get me wrong, I tried to hang in there because I thought she was the one. Okay, maybe I knew all along she wasn't the one but, oooh, she was fine as hell and I just wanted her to be. I kept thinking if I hung in there she'll change and eventually trust me. The only thing that eventually changed was my mind and I left her.

If I could talk directly to women and they would shut up and listen, I would seriously want them to know…

You're worth it! Plain and simple. You're worth all the good thoughts you can imagine. Life has enough cruelty without adding the drama of your friend's negative imagination into the equation of your relationship.

Why bring a good thing to an untimely demise. Obviously using the "five step program" does not work. If it did, there would not be so many break ups between couples.

Knowing yourself is the essential element to effectively embark upon a relationship. Other's self doubt places you in a position that makes you have equilibrium problems within your relationship. It is someone else's life you began to live the very moment you have others opinions. The hardest thing to do is to have your own opinion and trust it whole heartedly.

Why annihilate your own wants and needs by confusing them with the desires of someone who has absolutely nothing to do with what you're feeling.

Ladies before you ask others for advice you need to first ask yourself, does this woman you're asking advice from sleep next to your man and feel the heat of his warm skin on a cold winters night? Does this woman know how it feels when he kisses, caresses, and tantalizes your entire body with gentle touches of passion that only he alone can give? When he gives you money to go shopping, is it felt by your girlfriend? Therefore, try to remember when you talk to your girlfriends you have made the conscious decision to take advice from an empty shell. Someone who could not possibly, help you.

I say these things because this is where a woman needs to be when a man like me is pursuing her. When a woman knows these things, it will allow her to have a greater relationship with her man.

A woman with a great body and a weak, unintelligent mind does me no good. Eventually we will find that I'm unable to help her to be a better woman no matter how much I love her and she definitely can't help me become the great man I aspire to become.

I think it's time for me to interject because I don't want you younger men to think failure in a relationship is exclusive to the younger generation. It's not. Older men have also fallen victim to much of what you gentlemen have already spoke on.

But there comes a time when you need to…

...Just Get It Right (Mr. Robert)

Let me tell you a quick story. I knew a couple, Calvin and Doreen. They were married for eleven years, and had the perfect marriage. I wasn't the only one with that opinion. Everyone in our inner circle felt the same way. To us they were the model couple. They lived in a beautiful home with their four children and his elderly mother who suffered a stroke. One night his wife got sick and he took her to the emergency room. Shortly after their arrival she was diagnosed with a small viral infection that antibiotics could take care of with no problem. With her feeling better and him relieved they left the hospital. On the way home a drunk driver hit their car and Calvin was killed instantly. Doreen didn't have a scratch on her.

For the first two days after his death Doreen would not eat, sleep nor speak a word to anyone. Doreen just walked around looking at everyone like she was watching a movie. No reaction, what so ever, no tears, no laughter, just a blank look. On the third day Doreen came into the kitchen where everyone was eating breakfast. She was showered, dressed, smiling and greeting them all with a hearty good morning. Doreen kissed her sister Margaret and thanked her for coming over and being there for her family. Doreen grabbed her car keys and told Margaret she was going to the funeral home to make the final arrangements. Margaret offered to go with her, but Doreen said "no, this is something I need to do by myself". After several hours had passed Margaret got worried, but shortly after, Doreen walked in the door.

She told them "the funeral would be a week from Saturday; this will give everybody out of town a chance to get here". For the next five days Doreen managed to take care of her usual duties and tried her best to keep her children and mother-in-law's spirits up. On the sixth day when Margaret came over Doreen was sleeping late. Margaret tried to keep the kids from awakening their mother. But their youngest son went in the room anyway. He came back in the kitchen and Margaret noticed a strange look on his face. When she asked him what was wrong he replied; "I went to wake momma and ask her could I stay home from school but she wouldn't wake up." Margaret ran into the room and found Doreen dead. When the autopsy was done the doctors labeled her death natural cause. They could not find anything physically wrong.

Margret had the same funeral home that was holding the services for Calvin to pick up Doreen's body. The next day Margaret called the funeral home to make the arrangements. Margaret introduced herself and told the funeral director the nature of her call. He said, "Well Margaret, everything for your sister and her husband is already taken care of." "The obituary's are back also." "Would you like to come by and see them today?" Of course Margaret, being confused asked who made these preparations. "You did", replied the director. "The only thing you haven't given us is the death certificate from the coroner for your sister." Stunned, shocked, and clearly taken by surprise Margaret dropped the phone and passed out.

After Margaret regained consciousness, Doreen's mother-in-law gave Margaret a letter that was written by Doreen. The letter stated; on the second night after Calvin's death he came to me and said; I promised to never leave you alone and I've never broken a promise. I'm not going to start now. Not even in death. We belong together forever. Don't worry or be sad. I'll come and get you before the funeral. That's why she made her own arrangements. She wrote; he had never lied to her about anything. Even the things he knew would hurt her, he still told her the truth. She said all of her goodbye's in the letter and ended it with; tell my children daddy and momma are watching them from heaven so be good. I know they will believe what I say to them in this letter because we've always kept our word to them also.

We later found out when Doreen went to the funeral home she stopped at their storage unit and went through all their boxes until she found her wedding dress and his tuxedo they were married in. She placed Margaret's name on the bottom of her husband's insurance policy as the beneficiary in the event something happened to both of them. When she went to the funeral home she gave her name as Margaret and that both her sister and brother-in-law were killed in the car accident.

Now believe it or not this is a true story. At the funeral the officiating pastor was asked to read her letter. There was not a dry eye in the room. But for some reason they were tears of joy. I had never in my life attended a funeral like that. It truly felt like a celebration of their reunion with God. The same love they shared with family and friends in life was felt even stronger in their death. That day I became a believer in what is known as a "*soul mate*". People change but the soul doesn't.

No matter how many times I've told this story I always get the same reaction. It's unbelievable! But those of us who knew them learned that if you believe in something with all your heart it's going to happen. She had no reason not to believe him. He had never lied to her. His word to her was his bond. Even in his immortality.

After my divorce I believed, beyond a shadow of a doubt that I would never marry again. This one couple's life changed my mind. Now I don't know how she died no more than the doctors or anyone else. But, I can tell you true love does exist. There is another twist to this story.

Within four months of their death, nine couples who knew them were happily married. Their death also had its own profound effect on me. It appears the unpleasantness of my divorce faded and I found myself yearning for the type of affection that only exist between a man and a woman, in a committed relationship.

Don't get me wrong, the fear of getting hurt still exists but, I don't want to live the rest of my life alone. So I decided to search for the woman of my dreams. That's right I said dreams. Don't sit there and pretend we as men don't imagine the type of lady we want to marry. Other than a career, it is the most important decision we as men make. So, yes, I thought about what type of woman I wanted, needed and desired. I knew this was going to be a tough task, but, certainly well worth it.

Far too often, when men begin to think about having a mate, we start by mentally declaring what traits the woman must poses in order for us to choose her. It is for this reason I would like to share with you gentlemen what I believe is the major prerequisites for getting yourself ready for a serious committed relationship.

The process of preparing yourself for a partnership requires four levels of understanding. First, *recognize* no matter how perfect you think you are, you're not. When it comes to a relationship there's going to be adjustments that both of you need to make in order to fine tune your bond. Accepting this fact is the initial prerequisite in readying yourself for a mate.

The second level you must reach is, intentionally *understanding* what modifications you're prepared to undergo. For example; if she's been reading in bed because it helps her unwind and sleep better, but, you like to watch sports highlights on television while in bed before you go to sleep, how do you handle this simple situation? You see, it's usually the simple things that will test the changeability in a person's character. It is important to know what you are willing to compromise for a good rapport with your woman. Once you've decided which alterations you're prepared to give rise to means you've reached a twofold goal; a better understanding of one's self and a greater knowledge of the attributes you want and don't want in a companion.

The third level you must ascertain is *abilities*. When I say abilities I don't mean how great you are together sexually. I mean understanding what are your assets and proven potential to acquire. If you're a home owner, have proper transportation, formal education, financial stability, good credit, and you're saving to retire from your present employment and open your own business, your past accomplishments, are your assets. While your present situation and future plans are your proven potential. You have proven you can establish the things you want out of life and have the potential to reach further goals. Why would a person like you get involved with a woman who's assets are, bad credit, a rented apartment, over drafted checking account, no savings and when she speaks of her future plans, it's clear to you that even those plans will leave her welfare broke, financially destitute and emotionally unstable. With a women like this you know one of two things is going to happen; either you will be lead down the road to defeat or eventually you'll have to leave her in order to launch your future dreams.

The fourth level you must ascertain is *discipline.* Without it you will not be true to yourself or your woman. The best way to remain disciplined is to give careful consideration to anything you agree to because your word is your bond. YOUR WORD IS EVERYTHING! These are the four levels that you must reach within yourself first.

Unfortunately, some young men and women have been through more unhealthy relationships than we care to think about. These experiences will leave you feeling bitter and filled with self doubt. Which sometimes can and will cloud your judgment.

Therefore, if you're one of those men who has convinced himself that you'll adhere solely to the physical cravings and leave the emotional needs locked up in some imaginary vault. Eventually you'll believe in your own madness and ultimately end up with females you call *dips, quickies, my piece,* and a host of other names you give to your emotionally detached one night stands. But, just remember, late in the midnight hours when you're alone, your heart is no longer under protective custody against the invasion of the unwanted feelings.

Loving someone is the supreme significance of living a healthy, happy, and prosperous life. Sure there's going to be disappointments, and disagreements, leaving you feeling disenchanted. Basically, what this means is you'll go through life's normal cycle of up's and downs. But, I guarantee, that with or without being in a relationship, you'll go through these changes anyway. Why do it alone? Love in its brilliance will supersede all harnessed hurt, petty pride and judgmental jealousy. Find a woman who truly loves God first. This will give her great strength in self love that will spread directly to her man. Now I did not say find a woman who is religious. Loving God first has very little to do with religion.

To narrow down my main thoughts on this subject I'll just say…

Figure out if she's there to pick you up or knock you down? You will know if she's there to pick you up. She will motivate your every action. When you go to work she'll be the mental fuel you need to get up in the morning. But, if you find you have to argue with her to get the support you need to accomplish your goals, trust me she is there to knock you down. In this case run like hell and holla fire! But, if she's there to pick you up, you must give the same in return. Otherwise a good woman will eventually turn to someone else for support.

Make sure she deals with her emotions as they come and not anticipate them into existence with unnecessary thoughts that have no basis in reality. An insecure woman tends to have serious thoughts of dread. The problem is, the word dread simply means she's worrying about something that does not exist and it may not ever exist. Simply put she will drive herself crazy and you too. If your woman is not secure within herself, you will become a casualty in her world of total conflict.

There was once a belief that said; the easiest emotion to have is anger. Later in life I learned that anger was merely a byproduct of doubt. Self doubt is the true enemy.

I'd like for women to know that when she finds herself having too many conversations that sound like this: *I know I 'ain't got no business with this man. I know he's not what I need, but damn, he's definitely what I want. I need to walk away now from this hell I'm about to self inflict. I should let it go now, while I have not invested too much time and emotions.* One piece of advice; **HE'S NOT GOING TO CHANGE! LET IT GO!**

Gentlemen, when you say something to a woman. Remember they are your words and thoughts you're sharing with her. Once you say it to her, you cannot dictate how she's going to perceive what you just said. She can only understand from her own perception. Her understanding is from a different set of emotions. This is called individualism - the right to perceive from one's own understanding. Once you have told her what was on your mind, take the time to make sure you understand her take on what you said. This will stop a lot of confusion.

If any of what I've said helps you I'm happy. But out of everything I've tried to interject please don't lose these points. You must know yourself and remember your word is bond. Also, no matter how old you get change is inevitable. Bring God's wisdom and patients into your union and leave pride and petty judgment out of it. Right now, even at my age I'm working on my ability to adjust and change.

Yeah Mr. Robert I see what you're saying and I think you make great points as far as what we as men need to do to prepare ourselves for a woman but, with these females there's much change needed with them. What do you mean Tony? Some of their ways are too shallow.

Sometimes I just wonder if they have a pill for…

...MULTIPLE PERSONALITY DIS- OUT OF ORDER (Tony)

We all have multiple personalities. This is the natural order of life. We have developed a personality for when we are working, parenting, at church, housekeeping, partying, dating, etcetera. This is one of the most amazing characteristics of a human, their ability to be multifaceted. I've met women that are juggling a job, going to school, raising children, an active member of their church, managing their home, helping with needy family members and still maintain a healthy social life. These are not the women that I'm talking about. I'm speaking on the woman who has one job, maybe one or no children, lives with her parents, has very few bills and still can't seem to operate her private life in a well-designed manner.

These are the women that I always attract. Their main topic of a conversation starts with "*I'm just stressed out*". While she's saying this I'm looking at the outfit she's wearing; Dolce & Gabanna, Victoria Secret, Prada, Gucci, and diamonds by Tacori. Of course she's edgy and overwrought; she's wearing everybody's personality but her own. Where is her signature? Oh yeah, it's the one that say's I'm stressed from trying to afford all of these other peoples products. Now don't get me wrong, every woman should dress nice, but when designer clothes, specialized nail technician, certified pedicurist, and a professional hair stylist, takes precedence over necessity, she has multiple personality dis - out of order.

Their bedroom is filled with shoes, clothes and an assortment of other personal items lying around because she couldn't make up her mind about what to wear that day. She constantly screams the never ending question; "*have you seen my…?*" She pays more attention to her make-up application than she does her bills. Then to top it off, she runs late every morning and of course it's the kids' fault that she had to take a little time away from her beauty regimen to get them ready. When a woman puts more time, energy, effort and money into her physical appearance than she does her children and responsibilities, she has multiple personality dis- out of order.

When I see the signs of a woman being this way I grab my hat and run. It certainly is not because she is so called *"high maintenance"*, as most women with this disorder like to claim. It is for the simple fact she is dis-organized, discombobulated, and I quickly become dis-interested.

Yeah, she's good for a dip and an arm piece but, not for a wife. I don't mind sleeping with her, yet, somehow I don't see myself spending the rest of my life with a woman who's common sense has been dulled by the grandeur of her fashion sense. The amazing part about a woman like this is she works a job that can barely afford her life style. If she loves fashion so much it should be her career. Then at least she'll get paid for the advertising instead of giving it away at her expense.

The greatest thing I think a woman can do is live a life filled with honor and respect. It's typically the hardest thing to do. But, when you respect someone you won't lie to them or intentionally hurt them. A good woman will not contaminate the purity of their bond with lies. How can you say you love God but, tell lies to the person you lay next to every night. Please, tell the truth! When truth is our guide you can bet the relationship will grow in a manner that's constructive not destructive. I can't love a woman who lacks respect on any level.

I'm not only speaking of lying to her man. I'm saying don't lie to yourself. Why is it when women see a man's personality is a particular way, she will most of the time say he will change? No he won't. The science of psychology teaches us that the basic personality of a human is set by the age of five years old. What makes a woman think when she meets a man at age thirty five he's going to change? It's not going to happen! In this case she's lying to herself and she has him under the impression she's okay with who he is. Deceit is loves greatest enemy. The only thing you're going to get is a lot of frustration, heartache, and stress. Then to add insult to injury, she's going to tell herself another lie; it's all his fault. Just think of all the unhappiness that started over one simple little lie you told yourself; *he will change*.

I believe no one wants to be unhappy. However, I've seen quite a few women do the exact opposite of what it's going to take for her to be happy. I don't mean happy for a moment. I'm speaking of the type of happiness that lives in your heart. The kind you wake up with in the morning and go to bed with at night. This can only come from living a life without deceitful, manipulation. When some slick walking, fast talking man approaches her, she should love herself enough to see the truth. Not the smooth moves he's making on her. That surface he's showing her will soon fade and she'll be left with the part he tried to hide from her in the first place. Now don't get me wrong, a woman pulls the same bull on a man.

I've been on many dates that have left me in disbelief. I mean literally I walk away thinking; *did she really think I didn't notice the bullshit?* I realize for the most part women think we are unintelligent in the ways a woman pursues a man. But check this out; we're not! Not by a long shot. Let me give you a brief scenario;

Now, try to keep in mind I'm not saying this with any intent to insult, annoy or offend, but this is the truth that has been taught to me through the observation of many women.

When you ask a woman out on a date and she accepts, immediately she begins to plan what she is going to wear. Twenty to thirty minutes before date time or should I say show time, she touches her hair as she tilts her head at several different angles to make sure the style is flawless. She leans closer to the mirror image to make sure her cosmetic sculpting is supremely blended. The last glance of her face is the lip check. This is done by a carefully, calculated, multitude of twisting, stretching and pooching of the lips. Finally one big smile to ensure the lipstick has not infiltrated the brightness of her teeth and this concludes the face check.

Now she will take a couple of steps back from the mirror, and ever so gently run her hands down her dress while the hips, legs and waist perform the ritual body, sway and shake dance. A boost of the breast to make sure they are perched to perfection with just enough cleavage peeping out and the upper half is all set.

Now the booty check. This not only includes the mirror, but anyone else in the vicinity that can say if her butt looks to fat, flat or flawed. For some reason it appears the booty check is a group thing. Now, one good look back in the mirror and do the butt lift. This is done by standing on the tips of her toes then a slight lift of the booty. One look at the shoes and legs, front and back, and done. I truly believe women look in the mirror and say, "*mirror, mirror, I'm looking in, does my but look fat or does it look thin? Mirror, mirror, hanging there, will this outfit make the ladies jealous and the men stare?*"

I arrive to pick her up and her body is tight and the outfit is just right. I know, the first date for women is the flirting and teasing ceremony. This is where they eat very lady like and don't order anything that's going to taint her breath. Briefly she licks her lips in an alluring, welcoming manner. All of their movements are seductive, crossing their legs flaunting the thickness of her calves, while simultaneously revealing just enough thigh to be sexy yet respectable. She sits up straight to make sure she is displaying her breast like two trophies and her hand movements delicately flow.

Now gentlemen, we all know flirting is nothing new to us. We have mastered it into a fine art. Flirting to men is like riding a bike. Me myself, I get on and ride every chance I get. When I see a woman using flirtatious moves on me I say, let the games begin. I know when she crosses her legs, it is obvious she wants me to notice them; this is my cue to briefly glance down at her legs… then slowly look back into her eyes with a slight smile. This tells her I approve of what I see. When I see strategic movements of her hands, I touch and hold them as though they are as irresistible as she‘s presenting them. I purposely stare at her lips while she's licking them, then, I say playfully, stop doing that. Her response 99% of the time is; "stop what?" Then instantly she does it again. I move around in the chair as though I am adjusting myself due to over excitement. A slight pleased look comes across her face. Now she feels another one of her goals is accomplished. She feels I'm lusting for her.

She now believes her tactics are working. She's seduced me into a submissive state of mind with her dazzling, charm and beauty. She now feels in control. In other words I will do whatever it takes to have her body. Her confidence level increases by at least fifty percent and she's feeling great. News flash! I'm not under some hypnotic state of mind. I'm not hooked, sprung, or desperate. We just want women to feel comfortable, so we allow her to think she's in control. It's just what women need.

I grew up in a house with sisters, aunts, mother and a host of their female friends. I can tell when a woman is dressing to go out on a date with a man or kicking it with her girlfriends.

Why do ladies think men are stupid? Somehow women have convinced themselves our level of intelligence does not reach as far as the games they play. It has been my experience that sixty percent of the women I flirt with are going to give into something. Women know the same thing, if she flirts the right way eventually he's going to give into something. All humans have spontaneous genes in their bodies, it just depends on who can bring it out.

Man Tony, you right. These women think they are so slick. Man, you can see right through the bullshit. You feel me Brian? Absolutely Tony. Another thing Brian, as far as going out on a date, men have to prepare also. We have to choose something to wear. Get a haircut, make sure we know where were taking her just in case we need reservations. Now there is no way I'm going to pick her up in a dirty car. I get the car cleaned to perfection and make sure I show her the little things count to me. The entire time we're together I'm looking at her elaborate beauty from head to toe. I'm one hundred percent into her. As our evening comes to an end I'm really ready to love her and she says no. What the hell is that about? She says she wants to get to know me! Bullshit! Not when she's wasted all this time on our first date with games.

I spend fifty percent of my day working, twenty percent sleeping and twenty percent attempting to stay in touch with family and friends. I've only got so many hours during the week to devote to a woman until she and I get involved in a committed relationship. Truth be told, by the end of the first date a female already knows if she wants me or not. I certainly know if I've got a lady I want to pursue or just the freak of the week.

Here's my best advice for the ladies…

Give less energy to that one outfit to go out on that one date. Then you won't feel like he already owes you something because you spent your light bill money on the outfit that was designed to impress him. Because when the results are less than you expect you're bitter at him for your own failed plan. Once again, he did not mislead you, you mislead yourself.

Have enough confidence in yourself to show the real you unselfishly. Do not lie! Don't start the acquaintance off with games if that's not what you want in return. Emotions are not attached like your kidneys, liver, or lungs. They are entities that come and go through life.

Don't spend unnecessary time trying to control or change your man. Knowing who you are and what you want is a great enough task.

Respect is an identifiable term by which we all understand and relate to. Give it,

demand it, and don't settle for less.
Also, I'm so tired of hearing women say, *"no I don't want to have sex right away". "I would like to get to know you better".* That is one of the biggest lies I have ever heard. Women want to know what they're going to get before they get it. Stop It! Try having dates without the expectations list. This way you will be able to enjoy your evening minus the bullshit.

Remember when you go get a job you can't just tell them about your qualifications and they give you a check. You have to work for it. If you want a great man then, be willing to show him you're a great woman. Sex is not a game, don't play with it and it won't play with you.

Don't play the games they are not necessary. Save me the time, energy, effort and cash. Most of all save me the humiliation of the game. It emotionally destroys us as individuals. We all want a great relationship, but it takes great effort.

Tony have you seen those professional poker games on television? Yeah, Brian I've watched it. What does that have to do with women? Man, that's what dating is like. You have to constantly put on your poker face. Never let her see you sweat. Yeah, you're right. But, why haven't you gotten married yet? Brian, man fuck that, it's too hard. And any way Brian, how you gone ask me why haven't I gotten married, man why haven't you tied the knot? Shit, man you're older than me by a few years. Why won't you hang up your single boots, put on those slipper and slide into marriage?

Tony, I'm not going to lie. Nothing would make me happier. But, the reality of the situation is, it has to be the right one.

And believe me at this point in life I think…

…Ain't No Woman Like The One I Want.

(Brian)

Naw man, I just want a woman who is about it, not just talking about it. I'm so tired of hearing women say, "I need a man that wants more out of life". What they really mean is, I want a man that's willing to give me more out of life because, I don't want to put forth the effort to get it myself. I want women to stop saying shit they don't mean!

"I'm going to get in shape". That is the number one New Year's resolution made by women. *"I want tight thighs, small waist, perky breast and a tight ass".* They talk all that shit, while sitting in the fucking drive-thru of the nearest greasy hamburger joint, simultaneously ordering a double cheese burger, with all the trimmings, large fry, a cola, and by all means super size it. Stop saying it, if you don't mean it!

Man look at me! I play hard, laugh hard, fight hard and love even harder. I want what I give. I'm going to provide a woman with the full package. I want the same in return. No less. I'm like the Army; "I want a woman that can "be all she can be". I know these are the things required for positive, progressive, growth in a relationship with me.

Yeah well, Mr. Fucking total package, then why is it so hard for you to find the right woman? Alright Tony, keep talking shit, I'm gone give you two of these knuckles out of this package. Naw, but the reality of the situation Tony, is most women love the fantasy of a man like me, not the reality. I'm a spiritually guided, tall, dark, handsome, financially independent, gifted, man. When a woman sees the house, cars, and learns what I do for a living the fantasy is off and running in full force.

She usually tells me she'd like to get to know me better. This I don't believe either. For the most part I believe what she wants to know is, what's available for her to gain from me, as you said Tony. Women want to know what they're going to get before they get it. Then after a few dates she realizes being thin in the waist and fine in the face just won't be enough to keep a man like me. Then I hear that broken record *"you think you all that"*. If you translate that statement it really means; I want what you got but I'm not willing to do what it takes to get it. She wants me to make it easy for her to get what I've got. If you don't mean it, don't say it!

When a lady finds out she has to be one hundred percent woman to have a relationship with me, my reality, collides with her fantasy. The illusion is over. She can no longer live on the flight of her imagination. Her desire to be my woman diminishes. The reality of the situation is, she never wanted me, just her imaginary castle in the sky, and I love reality too much to live in the clouds of her imagination. If I could make women understand something it would be to work harder or desire less and don't say it, if you don't mean it!

The other topic I want to cover which maybe you gentlemen don't want to speak on is baby daddy drama. Aw man I feel you on that shit! Nobody mentioned that bull! I'm gonna tell you Derrick I'm also a single father. There are times that baby, momma, drama, exist. But, when I'm spending time with a lady, I do everything humanly possible to avoid it from infecting our time together. Unfortunately, some ladies I've dated who are single mothers allow baby daddy drama to become a part of our date far too often. Man Brian, you ain't never lied, go ahead preach brother! Tony I get so tired of sitting at a nice quiet dinner and she's sitting there text messaging, telling him to stop calling her. Then she has nerve enough to turn to me and say *well I have to talk to him because he's got the baby*. Shit, if you couldn't trust him with the child then you should have gotten a baby sitter. I'd rather pay for a sitter than go through this bullshit. He ain't doing shit but cock-blocking! Furthermore, if it has to be like that, then on the nights he has visitation just don't go out with me. Shit, stay home and answer all his calls! That's what I'm talkin bout Brian! That's just how I feel about it! Then you feel me Charles? Oh hell yeah! Go ahead Brian, spit that truth!

Charles I honestly don't mind listening to the issues she faces in her life as a single parent and if there is something I can do about it, she won't have to ask. But, after I've had to calm her down every time we get together because her baby daddy has made her angry, after a while I feel like I'm dating him. Not her. Life is too short for all the drama. Please, save the topic of his latest performance for her girlfriends! Oh yeah, let's not forget the statement she makes at the end of all of her raging complaints; *"I'm through with all his bullshit"*. Yeah, right. Don't say it, if you don't mean it.

I'm not saying that a woman has to be perfect. This is not the intention of my statements at all. What I'm saying is she has to live everyday as though she wants to win at life. Give each day her best. Sure we all have those moments when we take a day off and simply relax. Okay. Then make it the best day of relaxation you know how to have. Don't half relax today and tomorrow say, "*But I didn't get a chance to relax; I didn't actually do what I wanted to yesterday"*. Take the day off from everybody and everything. Just spend the day doing what you want and do it to the fullest, or don't say it, if you don't mean it!

I work hard every day and night to develop myself to the fullest, spiritually, mentally, emotionally and financially, in that order. If I have a wife who is not as tenacious with the development of her complete self as I am then strong conflict is automatic.

Another thing that pisses me off about some women is they claim they want independence. Okay, I'm a man who firmly believes a woman should be independent. But the minute I respect her independence she say's; "*but if you cared you would have tried to stop me*". What in the hell do they think independence is? This means you're ready, willing, able and more than capable of handling the decisions you make in your life. I am not here to save her from herself. When she makes a decision to do something, it does not matter if I like it or not. My job as her man is to accept and respect her right to choose. Not impose some type of sanction on her ability to think for herself. I will give her my opinion but, only if she asks. Even then I still want her to come to her own conclusion. I don't have all the inside information on what it is she wants to do or even the motivation behind why she wants to in the first place. But, she does. Therefore, it is in her best interest to make the decision for herself. This way no regrets are made from *I should have*, which to me, are the worst regrets anyone will ever suffer. One thing for sure some of the greatest things in life have come from not being sure but trying it anyway. Besides, I don't want a woman I have to raise. Don't say it, if you don't mean it.

I want ladies to know…

If you want the complete package: Then come on full your damn self. Or at least be ready to reach your full potential through plain old hard work and diligence. Men like me will not settle for anything less in a wife. It would be unfair to our future.

Learn the difference between what feels good to you and what's good for you and please draw the line when you start settling for good enough.

Don't expect your man to know what you want and think. Hell, sometimes he doesn't know what's going on in his own mind. Make up your mind as to what you want, and then express it as clearly to him as possible. And if you don't mean it, don't say it.

Don't let past relationships interfere with present dates. You will surely miss out on the best a person has to offer if you're constantly living in the past emotionally.

There are several great brothers out there who are ready, willing, and able to get in a committed relationship. Stop saying there isn't any good men out there. There are plenty. Have you ever wondered why you haven't got one? Give it some serious thought.

I'm listening to all you brothers and I agree with what you gentlemen are saying but y'all ain't hit the real issues for me. I just wish there was a…

...Love and Sex Depository (Winston)

You know like a bank. Except at this bank you would deposit some of those tender, affectionate moments you have at the beginning of the relationship and save them for the days that misery is inevitable. This way when my woman decides she's going to be angry with me for the night, I'll just go straight to the reservoir, fill out a withdrawal slip for one hot, steamy, night of sex and enough honey I love you, to last for a couple of days while my woman's going through the uglies.

Oh wait! My bad, there is such a place. As a matter of fact there are several of these places located right outside your door. Who knows, depending on the type of associates your woman has, they may be found right in your home disguised under the title of, her best friend. Just pick a spot, the club, grocery store, work, church, or even driving down the street.

Okay, y'all think it's funny, but truth be told this is the epitome of cheating. We have all heard it said many times; "*the heart wants what it wants*". When I come home and my spirit is full of passion and romance I want to share these feelings with my woman. But, if my woman's in the frame of mind for an argumentative, upheaval, I realize enthusiastic passion is out of the question. Therefore, while she's lashing me with the wrath of her tongue, it may appear that I'm listening but, my mind is slowly drifting toward the depository.

Even if my girl say's not tonight. I'm too tired. That's how she feels. On the other hand, I feel like making love. Occasionally I'll go without a passionate night of sex but, it ain't gonna happen too many nights in a row. I might play with myself. Aw, man don't y'all sit there and act like I'm the only one. Shit man you can act crazy if you want to but I'm gone be happy.

That's what life's about. Women do it too. That's why half the time you can't find the batteries to the remote control. Then she blames it on the kids, saying; *"well I'll be damn, the kids have been playing with this remote again."* No I'll tell you what happened. I came home from work early and she didn't have time to put them back in the remote. Okay, if you don't believe it then explain to me how is it, she can always get up and find two little double AAA batteries in a huge house? Answer that one for me. Ah ha, never thought about that have you? Man Winston you funny as hell! Honestly Derrick, the truth is always funnier than fiction. But, on the real, it's rare that I'm going to take matters into my own hands, literally. Please believe it. Generally, I'll find a woman who wants the same thing I want.

Winston, you gone put that out there just like that? Hell yeah Derrick! Men and women are equally equipped and morally obligated to the safe keeping of their emotional stability, happiness and well being. When a woman consistently shrugs off my needs as though they are hers to direct, you can bet I'll find a depository and make a withdrawal. I guarantee.

Hey Winston, what happens when you get caught? Derrick I ain't gone lie. That has happened. Well what did she do? Aw shit man you know the deal. My girl got a severe case of the uglies. She started screaming to the top of her lungs, calling me plenty of names accompanied by adjectives. Black motha-*&#*&, no good, piece of, well you get the idea. She started breaking shit throwing her arms around in the air like she was directing rush hour traffic. I let her rant and rave for a while then I said, you've got to be kidding me! You got everything you wanted! You did everything you wanted to do! Her response was, *"WHAT!" "See, I know you have lost your damn mind now!"* "Do you want to know the truth?" *"Yeah Winston, tell me the truth, I can't wait to hear this* *bullshit!*" That's when I brought reality to light.

Whenever you go out of town with your girlfriends don't I support your decision to go? Every time you go shopping with your girlfriends, I make sure you got money? Don't you go bar hopping with your girlfriends whenever you want? Don't you go to ladies night, with your girlfriends? Don't you go to all the, my girlfriend got her heart broken, let's get drunk and male bash, night out with my girlfriends? Didn't you go to the; my girlfriend just got divorced celebration? Don't you go to the health club with your girlfriends? Don't you go to Sam's club with your girlfriends? Don't you go to your book club with your girlfriends? Name one time I ever tried to stop you from doing what you wanted! Now you're angry! Please! Forgive me for supporting you in all of your endeavors! And by all means, forgive yourself for being so narrow minded and arrogant as to believe that I would actually suffer and do without simply because you decided to treat our relationship as though it was some kind of play date! What did you think I was doing? That's just it, you didn't think about me at all! As long as you were doing what you wanted to do and nothing was interfering with the part of your imagination that said you had your man in check, you was all good! That's all that mattered! The only reason you're sittin here with a case of the uglies is simply because you don't like the byproduct of your own decisions!

Now Tony, you've known me most of our lives right? Right, Winston? Well then you know for a fact I've never been a person to argue or carry a grudge. You're absolutely right Winston. I will always try to get to the solution end of a situation as expediently as possible. I can't stand to constantly deal with unnecessary anger or upheaval. Right! Right, Winston, but what happened after you told her all of that? So right away I quickly explained to her in a calm cool manner, that in order for the healing process to begin she must take responsibility for her part in our injured relationship. *"You take responsibility for your part, you lying, cheating whore!"* So without delay and deepest, sincerity I said, I'm sorry and I was wrong. But she just kept raising hell. *"Going out with my girlfriends ain't shit like fucking somebody else!"* Then I said; I agree. But, if you continue this pattern of anger and denial then you could destroy any possibilities of you and I reaching some equitable agreement. We need to do what it takes to mend our relationship and grow from the experience.

But, instead of saying, well Winston I'm gonna need some time alone. She just kept on with all the name calling, crashing shit to the floor and getting in my face. Then I just told her flat out, the only thing this displaced anger is going to get you is a misplaced relationship! And this anger will be replaced with an emotion better known as, my man done gone and left me blues. Then I had to call the police on her.

Winston you're crazy as hell! Oh y'all laughing. Shit, I can laugh now. But that shit wasn't amusing while it was happening. I had to have her locked up, go to court and deal with a lot of legal bullshit. Only for her to come back home anyway. That's what pisses me off with women. They go through all that drama, knowing they're not going to leave. When a woman's gonna leave you, she doesn't perform like that. Because she's already decided in her mind, you're not worth all that effort.

Okay, Winston, I think you've made us laugh enough for one day. Okay, Mr. Robert.

On a serious note, if you could tell women something that you honestly believe will help them have a better understanding in a relationship, what would that advice be…

When you're angry save the theatrics, get some space to think before you react, if at all possible. Remember some things you can't undo.

A lot of men feel inept when their girl is cheating. They question their own ability to satisfy her. This is where the real anger comes from. He feels less than the man he thought he was. To me it's no different for a woman. When a woman finds out her man has been deceitful, she is first angry with him but the real anger is within herself. She now has to question her own abilities and step up her game or she knows it will happen again.

When is one woman enough? When she decides she's the one. When she is willing to do what it takes to be with that man. It sounds simple but unfortunately it's not. The human spirit is not designed to stay the same; if you think back to when your favorite thing was hanging out with your friends and riding your bike. Now you may still like hanging out with your friends but you most certainly are not going to leave the club and hop on your ten speed bike and roll on to the crib. At least I hope not anyway. Ladies keep up with the changes in your man's life. Don't look the other way when you first see things going wrong. You will always know when his normal routine begins to change. They may be small alterations but pay attention anyway.

A relationship to me can be described as a team. The man and woman, these are the immediate team players. Children, mothers, fathers, sisters, brothers, are your second string; friends and other family members can only watch from the sideline. Never take advice from the people on the sideline. And only give a small amount of consideration to the second string. You must remember only the immediate team members are truly privileged to all the plays.

A woman must know her role in a relationship. Just as a man must have a clearly defined role as well. Now I'm not saying things don't or can't change, you can bet they will. But, don't change the play in the middle of a game without first consulting your team mate. If you should decide to do this you need to understand you just stopped being a team and became an I. You will lose the team. You should first consult with your major player.

One of the greatest things a woman can do for her man is know his moods. If she knows this, she'll be able to communicate effectively. To me a great relationship is two people on the same path. If this is the case finding out one another's moods are essential for a progressive, loving, sensual, healthy, relationship.

The best time to get a yes answer from a man is during sex. This is the time a woman's bargaining power with a man, is at an all time high.

For a woman to consistently ignore vital information regarding what makes her man happy sends a signal to him that says she is only interested in what she can get from him. As opposed to what she can get with him.

Ladies the three greatest secrets a man keeps from his woman is: How much money he makes. Men don't tell how much cash he has access to because he will be subjected to total accountability. She will be able to say, "*What did you do with all that money.*" No man wants to hear that.

The second thing is, if he's cheating. He won't tell her for fear of losing his good thing.

The third and most important is telling a woman his greatest fear. Whatever that is varies from man to man. If a woman knows this she could attack him with his own weakness. This is too risky. He knows it will leave him far too vulnerable.

At the same time there are things that a man would love to open up and talk about with his woman. For example: “past relationships”. Sometimes I want to tell my woman about another woman so she can either step up to the plate or make sure she doesn’t make the same mistakes or maybe it’s simply for bragging rights. This is why it is so important for a man and a woman to be great friends before lovers.

Men would love to talk openly about her family. However, women get so uptight when you don’t like their family members especially when they’re close knit.

I believe my woman is the first face I see in the morning and the last face I see before I fall asleep. I want to look at her at least seventy percent of the time and feel in my soul that God made her just for me. If you don’t feel this way about your mate at least sixty percent of the time, maybe you should rethink your situation.

There is something called common sense. Use it. Don't be afraid to utilize that great attribute. If you don't like the way things are going, change it. But remember the change can only begin in you. Then if he's worthy of having you, he will take heed and make the necessary adjustments. However, if he isn't, it's time for you to take your efforts and transfer them inward and leave.

Man Winston I know exactly what you're talking about when you say "*know your mates moods*". You feel me Derrick. Yeah man and I'd like to take it a step further and say…

...KNOW WHAT IS REQUIRED BEFORE YOU GET HIRED (Derrick)

A relationship between a man and a woman is like nurturing a plant. You must know the requirements or without a doubt, it will shrivel and die. When you meet a woman she could be a beautiful flower with flourishing buds just waiting to bloom. But, if you don't know that she requires lots of sun, plenty of water and pruning four times a week, slowly but surely, she will breathe her last breath. Her buds will suffocate, refuse to open, and transform into a hideous, ball of blackened, dry, crust; leaving her unresponsive, without possibility of thriving under your careless, remiss, ever again. The once vibrant woman you knew will cease to exist, never again to be seen. Of course I'm speaking metaphorically. I'm trying to keep the language clean and respectful. Oh, I'm glad you said something Derrick because I was wondering what the hell you were talking about. Real funny, Prentice. It's okay now Derrick, You can keep going since I understand what all that was about. The exact same thing happens when a woman is uninformed of the necessities of her man. He will start off with long, thick, stems aligned with vigorous, green leaves. Now the requirements may be to trim his stems daily, clip his leaves, moderate sunlight and large quantities of water. But, when you don't trim the stems the vines will become untamed, and grow in a wild uncontrollable manner. The leaves in search of water will stray and eventually break away from the vines leaving nothing more than limp, lifeless, strands of good for nothing shadows of what used to be.

Knowing a person's requirements is key to a long lasting, healthy relationship. When a man or woman is void of their partners basic necessities it is there you will find shattered love. This sounds simple but it's not. Often times we are so engulfed in our own world of issues, dreams, problems and afflictions from past relationships that finding the brain space to become concerned about someone else's needs become virtually impossible.

For the most part it's not that we don't know what our mate wants or needs, we're simply just too busy with something or someone else at that particular time to give a damn. We live in a selfish society that says; I got mine and I'm too busy trying to keep it. Finding the brain space to think about the needs of our mate seems to just stress us out even more.

I remember one day my wife came to me and said she wanted to talk about something that was on her mind. I had just gotten off work and was tired as hell. She started off by saying "*I'm not happy*". Well that's all she got out before I snapped. I said, what do you mean you ain't happy? I go out here every day and bust my ass working overtime, trying to keep a roof over our head! Look in every room of this house and show me one thing that was free! This house cost money and everything in it required cash! Let me just lay it out for you, it took paper to get it and it takes paper to keep it! Now you say you ain't happy! Well maybe you'll be satisfied with one of those men who's unemployed, on drugs and steals from you every chance he gets! I can't deal with this bullshit right now! I'm doing the best I can! Once I completed my motivational speech on how much I wasn't interested in what she had to say, I noticed she was staring at me with such a confused facial expression. She said, *"all I was going to say is I'm not happy with you taking chances driving that raggedy ass car to work every day and I was wondering if you thought we could afford to get you a new vehicle, but fuck you. Now I'm about to go in this kitchen that cost you, to eat some food that cost you, then lay in the bed that cost you and I bet you got a pretty damn good idea of how much that statement you made, just cost you".*

Aw man, y'all ain't got to laugh that hard!

You had to feel dumb as hell? Yeah, I did Mr. Rick. Even though I felt like shit afterwards, I still told myself it was okay that I went off because, I'm just plain old tired and don't give a damn about what she had to say anyway. I also told myself that if she wasn't bitching all the time I would not have been so quick to get angry. These were just a few of the things I thought of, to justify my cynical behavior and stroke my own ego. But, the truth of the matter is, I was wrong.

All I'm trying to say is, I don't think it's so difficult for us to understand one another's needs or wants. But, far too many times when a man feels he's not living up to his own expectations he stays on the defensive because he already feels inadequate. Not only is a man aware of his deficiencies so is his woman. She is fully aware of when her man is more psychologically vulnerable. But she will attack him with comments like, *"you sorry mother&%##@%m !" "You can't even pay the bills up in here!"* Then she hits below the belt with this statement; *"And you call yourself a man!"* As a rule men are strong enough to physically beat a woman down with little or no effort. But a woman's mouth, pound for pound, will say words to her man that instantly slashes his man hood to shreds and injures his soul. When his woman goes there, it's virtually impossible for a man to forget those words. He may forgive but he won't forget. The worst part is, it may appear that he's turned the other cheek. But he didn't. Trust and believe, when he gets back on top of his game, he's going to make her wish she'd never made those statements.

Once she's said those things to him, the next move is for him to go out and find someone to lick his wounds. I believe the number one reason men cheat is because the other woman is not aware of his failures. He knows a new woman can only see what's on the surface, a man driving a brand new car, sharp clothes, and some money in his pocket. Believe me he's not going to tell her the car note is two months past due and ain't no insurance on it. The credit card that he purchased that suit on is maxed out and the money in his pocket is supposed to be for the mortgage note. Why would he want to tell the truth? He's out trying to get a drink and a dream not a sequel to his nightmare. We're telling her how our wives don't understand a good, hard working man and that all he wants is a woman that can appreciate him. We tell her whatever she needs to hear not limited to telling her he and his wife are getting a divorce.

Derrick man you know you're telling all the truth. So tell us what advice you can give to women that will help them to keep peace in their relationship, especially in today's economy when you know even the above average man is being hit hard financially.

Well Mr. Rick I'd tell them…

Ladies should be aware of what is going on with a man before she decides to get in a relationship with him. Women are just as aware of the issues that are going on in society right now. Do not fool a man into believing you understand and you've got his back, when in reality what you're thinking is, it's going to be easier on you while he struggles through these challenging times. Please know what is required, before you get hired.

If you need a man to make a certain amount of money in order for him to facilitate your needs; please, let him know what is required before he gets hired. Don't bring him on board only to tell him later, what he has is not good enough. You are asking for a catastrophe.

Last but not least, we all have those moments when were just plain old sick and tired of our mate and we don't care if they go away forever. This is a false emotion that goes away over a short period of time.

When you experience this type of feeling remember you are being consumed with your own world. It's okay. Just take a little time away from the situation so you can get a clearer picture. As opposed to the one that's clouded with shades of stress and disappointment.

Derrick, I can honestly relate to the statement you made about, men saying whatever women want to hear, to get what they want. Although, women are guilty of this same crime, men tend to make it far more misleading with those…

...PROMISES, PROMISES
(Prentice)

I consistently attempt to tell the truth. Yet, somehow the truth is never good enough. You don't believe me? Check this out. When I tell a woman at the beginning of our dating process that I'm not interested in a committed relationship, instantly she becomes cold. Of course this will never do. So this topic that I'm speaking on is totally directed to the ladies. Y'all ain't got to ask me what I can tell the ladies that will help them have a better understanding of their relationship. Y'all know I'm a fool! I'm gone tell it like it is! Therefore I'm about to carry on a full blown conversation with women who are not even here. Because they need to understand how important this is!

A woman wants to have ear sex. That's right I said ear sex. She wants to hear all the things that turn her on, or better yet, all the things she wants to hear. Ear sex is the most precious commodity a man can posses when it comes to dating a woman. Truly, if you don't have money tell her about a potential plan and whisper it in her ear the right way and you've got yourself a date, sex and a good woman that will stick by your side until she realizes she's been ear fucked.

Ear fucking is a powerful tool used by men to capture the attention of a woman. Its sole purpose is to seduce her into getting what he wants, simply by saying the things she wants to hear. Ladies should stop enjoying ear fucking so much and we would not be able to get away with the things we get away with. Women should pay more attention to his actions. If he says he's not working right now but he's looking for a job, watch how diligently he gets up every day and pursues employment. Check out his resume. See how often he's called for interviews. In other words do your homework. Don't allow ear fucking to get in your way.

Here is another prime example of ear fucking. *You're so beautiful.* This may be true, but understand you're still stunning regardless if he tells you or not. Of course it's flattering to hear but, remember it's still just words, a simple compliment; Nothing more.

I think I'm falling in love with you. Of course this may be true but, if she can't contact him in the late night hours and he's disregarding her needs, please remember you're being ear fucked. Falling in love with someone means you're putting forth every effort to make it work. Again pay attention to his actions not his words.

I need to be with you. No other woman makes me feel like you do. Well of course. This is the deep down ear fucking. Sure it makes her feel elated and special. But, this is simple knowledge; no two human beings are the same. We don't walk the same, talk the same, nor perceive things the same.

We do not have identical chemical composites. We are different in our biological make-up; also our mental and physical attributes are dissimilar. Most of all, it's humanly impossible for us to experience the same thing; therefore, no two women are the same. So remember when he says, *no other woman makes him feel the way you do;* this is a simple truth, even if he never tells you. This is common sense. Ladies need to know its okay to be grateful for the compliment but live by the truth.

Now when a woman hears a man say; *you make me want to be a better man and I don't know what I'd do without you.* The one hundred watt light bulb should go off in your head. Stop! Think about it! When did she meet him? If he was already 40 or older what the hell did he do up until he met you? Ladies need to take their ego out of the way. She needs to stop thinking she's Neo, she is not the one. Trust me, if he's making adjustments for a better life, it's because he is at the point where he's personally made the conscious decision to redefine his world. This is why he chose her in the first place. She fit the profile for what would suit his world at that time. It's okay to feel special but always understand the truth.

Here's one that should really blow your mind. This is said when a man starts to hit that inner ear or the G spot of the ear. *You're the only one who gets my dick this hard.* If you believe this then by all means add to your belief factors that you're the only woman who has ever, ever, ever, ever, ever, ever, ever, made him reach a climax. Dick get's the same kind of hard it's going to be whenever he's about to reach a climax. I'm not trying to burst a woman's bubble. I'm just attempting to help ladies make clear cut decisions based on proven physical experience as opposed to the process of ear fucking. Oh, and by the way, I'd like to do a survey on how many babies were conceived by women listening to a man saying; *I'm only gone to stick the head in.*

Men sit in clubs and make bets on who can ear fuck the best. I swear! I got a friend who is the king of ear fucking. Damn, this man ain't had a job in eight years but he always gets the best women. And, let's not talk about construction workers. When women walk by, the workers see who can ear fuck a woman the best. Most of the time ladies stop and give them their number and half the time they don't even want it. It's just a game to liven up their time at work. They're talking shit. You're listening to shit. Now what do you expect to get?

Ladies should listen to his words. But, take only his actions to heart. This is what ladies need to do in order to keep unnecessary garbage out of their life. When she dilutes the power of ear fucking, she will empower herself to get past the bullshit and into the truth of who she's really dealing with almost immediately.

You know what makes ear fucking so destructive? When everything is over, she realizes her hurt is over nothing. That's right I said nothing. Simple words that added up to a bunch of lies she decided to fall for. Then she finds herself sitting saying, *"but he said he was gonna leave his wife". "He said he was gonna marry me as soon as he was making more money".* No matter what the story, it all boils down to full blown deceit by way of ear fucking. It cuts you in a place where no pill can heal, time can't cure, money won't move, and prayer ain't fair. This grief is now the veracity of your life. It's yours, all yours. You can't give it away. Nope, it's yours. And forget about sleeping it away, the pain wakes you up just to remind you, its still there.

I'm familiar with this excruciating pain. Because this is exactly how I felt when I allowed my ear and her mouth to have a relationship. She said all the right things, at all the right times. Even though we couldn't be together most of the time, it was okay because she told me; *"soon, we will be together"*. *All I had to do was hang in there.* She said" *baby look at the big picture"*. The things she said to me should have been put in the Ear Fucking Hall of Fame. Shit, we even had phone sex. I only wish since my ear had most of the fun, it should have been the one to hurt. But nooooo. Even in the midst of my pain, I found myself saying; "if I could just hear her voice'. I was like a junky. I was hooked on a three times a day, ear fucking habit.

So I've only got one real piece of advice for you ladies…

GETTING EAR FUCKED CAN GET YOU PREGNANT AND EVENTUALLY YOU'LL GIVE BIRTH TO NOTHING BUT A PAINFUL SHORT STORY! REMEMBER, ACTIONS SPEAK LOUDER THAN WORDS! DON'T LET YOUR TWO EARS GET YOUR ONLY HEART IN TROUBLE!!!

Well Prentice, I want to say something but I have to stop laughing first. Okay. Okay. Okay! You alright Mr. Chico? Yeah. Yeah. I'm straight. Prentice, you're just crazy! A stone fool! What you got to say Mr. Chico?

Well I guess it's my turn to share some helpful information. I have to confess when we first decided to do this little barbecue and discuss women I thought it was going to be chaotic to say the least. But I must honestly say, I've enjoyed listening to all of your stories and suggestions. So now let me see if I got all of this right.

Kenneth wants a woman to return to the clearly defined eloquence of the ladies in the past.

Mike wants them to trade in their balls for a king,

Dave wants them to stop dropping it like

it's hot and pick up some self respect.

Charles wants them to get off the sister hot line and start thinking for herself.
Tony wants them to take the cure for the designer disease and stop with the useless games.

Brian wants them to put up or shut-up.

Robert wants everybody to just get the shit right.

Winston, you want women to know when she's not, somebody else is.

Charles, you want women to drop the destructive words and pick up some much needed patients.

Prentice, with your crazy ass, you want women to stop enjoying ear action so much.

Have I covered everything so far?

Why y'all laughing? I'm just summarizing what all of you said. Yeah but the way you put it makes it sound funny as hell! Well Charles, I ain't trying to be funny, I just want to make sure I got it, that's all. Well I'd say you summed it up pretty good. Alright Kenneth, I just want to make sure I'm keeping up, being old school and all. The only thing I have to add to the points of issue is…

...What You See Is What You Get. Watch, Listen And Learn (Chico)

My life's story, when it comes to women begins with, if I could just find the right woman. I would be faithful and the happiest man in the world. However, I don't journey anywhere; I think holy matrimony is waiting to greet me. I believe there's a bacteria in me that renders me immune to staying in a relationship over long periods of time.

Some men have made up their mind to never marry. I'm one of those men. Besides, you know that old saying, "*why buy the cow when you can get the milk free*". Most of the time I don't have to *go* see the woman to get the milk. She delivers it to my door. I call it no hassle dating.

The amazing part of this is the only reason I've been so successful in dating in this manner is because most women don't realize their own power. Whenever I hear a man say women are the weaker sex, I recognize right away he's the type of man who has to envision women weak in order to boost self confidence in his own libido. Any man who considers himself knowledgeable regarding women will quickly tell you women are one of the most powerful creatures God has placed on this earth. I'm just glad most women don't recognize it. If women knew the magnitude of their power, most men would not get to second base without tightening up their game.

Fortunately, for men like me, most women are unaware of their ultimate supremacy. What do you mean Chico? Well Charles, women have great powers and they know it, or at least they should know it. First and foremost when a woman is getting ready to go out, she dresses for a dream. She knows she will attract the male with her physical appearance. She walks into a room and right away her mere presence commands attention. Now here's the thing, all men see different things when they look at a woman. One man may see her as having sexy legs, another her breast, waist or face. But none the less whatever it is, women are the initiator with nothing more than her presence. The male becomes aroused and approaches her. While he talks to her she will watch, listen and learn. After a short conversation with him she will trust her instincts and identify what's going on with him and act accordingly. She decides if he's worthy of further conversation or push him away and wait for the next man to step to her. Power number one: the ability to command and choose, what man will and will not have the honor of her company.

However, this is usually not the case. If I had the opportunity to speak with women I'd honestly tell them; they don't understand their powers. Women don't watch, listen and learn. And they don't trust in their own instincts.

Ladies give men powers they don't really have. It's all in a woman's imagination or shall I say her desires. When a man meets a woman he wants her to fulfill his fantasies Ladies automatically know just what the doctor ordered. This is why she starts off by filling his fantasy prescription. They wear the sexy bras, thongs, garter's and girdles. They put weave on and rip wax off. Whatever she can put on or take off, in order to feed his fantasy frenzies she does it; all of this with the hope that she will be the one. Major Power number two: the ability to reinvent herself to satisfy her man. Men can't do that. What you see is what you get. And if he comes to bed with thongs on, beware. Stop laughing; you know I'm telling the truth.

Women are also automatically in tune to his emotional needs. She knows a man becomes frightened if he feels he has not pleased her sexually. She is fully aware of his hopes before they ever encounter the sheets. His expectations are to satisfy her sexually. Gentlemen I know you can relate strongly to what I'm about to say. No matter how confident a man talks, when it comes to the actual act, he is never sure, especially when it's his first time with her. Now here's the thing that makes women geniuses: if he does not please her sexually she must keep it to herself. Because she knows it can cut him down into a pile of pathetic, useless, meat and emotionally damage his ego and the possibility of any kind of relationship is out the door. This is why women fake so many orgasms. Power number three, the ability to satisfy his need to be a great lover even when he's not. Men can't do that, again what you see, is what you get.

A woman basically controls the entire tone for the relationship. She knows how to hypnotize him with his own freaky, fantasies and captivate him by way of sensual satisfaction. When you add mental and physical together this equals ecstasy. These are her natural abilities. Men do not posses those extraordinary gifts. As I said before, what you see is what you get. A man must be in tuned to her mentally. This is the only way a man can truly satisfy a woman. He too must watch, listen and learn, in order to keep her happy. Believe it or not men are more afraid of a one on one relationship than women. Because, when a woman decides to leave a man she takes with her, his fantasies, (mental), and sexual strength, (ego). She can shut him down completely. But a woman on the other hand simply reinvents herself for the next man. Shit I know some guys that have never recovered from the loss of their woman.

Well Mr. Chico, this explains why you've never been married. Now you're getting the big picture. And I'm going to go out on a limb here and guess that's why you're not married either Brian. That's right. My Momma told me *"son any woman that can make you, can break you"*. Brian I'm not afraid to admit my fears and one of them happens to be getting hurt. I used to say I'm too young to fall in love. Now I say I'm too old for a broken heart.

Women may not recognize their power but I do. When a man and a woman get in the bed and she say's *not tonight dear I have a headache.* His ears heard exactly what she said. But, his ego heard; *I don't want you sexually.* Right then and there he begins experiencing a major melt down. He's not angry because of the lack of sex; he sees it as she has just used her powers to rob him of his manhood with one tiny little two letter word. NO! When you take sex from a man you've taken away his reason for breathing. When a woman says no, she's tampered with his mind set that told him he was in control of her body. The part of his imagination that said, she wants him as much as he wants her.

This is one of the reasons men cheat. It's to feel like someone needs and wants them sexually. It's their feeble attempt at gaining back their control. It's not about the sex, it's about the control. Trust me; what you see is what you get.

Men are very insecure when it comes to physical interaction with their woman. I have chosen not to leave my emotions tied up in one blanket. I know my strengths and weaknesses. Some men are easily pleased sexually however, it depends on their sensual level. Women must realize sex is vital to a man's existence. I know for a fact sex is an essential part of my well being. Men are conquers by nature. When he thinks you're taking away his prey, he will come out fighting. That's why when a man and a woman ain't having consistent sex, their having constant fights.

This is what I want women to understand…

When it comes to a man please believe, what you see is what you get!

Make sure you become great friends before sex ever enters into the equation.

Know your powers that dwell within. Then do not be afraid to use them. They are there to help you make better decisions. Don't look for a man to have those mystical abilities. It's not going to happen. What you see, is what you get!

Know that some men are going to cheat regardless of what you do. That's why it's important for you to use your power of intuition by getting to know a person first and become friends. This will allow you to make better decisions before entering into a committed relationship.

A man will less likely cheat on a woman when he has the total package consisting of: trust; knowing what it takes to please one another physically; understanding the mental aspects of your partner and respect. These four things together produce what is known as Maximum Happiness and Ultimate Sex!!!

For those of you who don't know me I'm Mr. Rick. I'm glad I've had this opportunity to see and hear you gentlemen get together and air your concerns about women and relationships. You guys have taught me that when it comes to women and men in relationships, there truly is no generation gap.

Therefore, I feel it my duty to rap this social event up by sharing with you what seventy years of experience will bring to your life. First, it's going to bring peace of mind. This is because you will learn to simplify your thought process. You will not cloud your mind with unnecessary drama. You know Chico, yeah, what's up Rick? Listening to you talk reminded me of an interview I did years ago. The interviewer asked me a hypothetical question, she said; Mr. Rick, if you had a daughter and throughout her entire life you could only give her three pieces of advice regarding relationships, what would you tell her?

I said…

…YOU WILL ONLY GET WHAT YOU GO AFTER (Mr. Rick)

This was the hardest question for me to answer because the greatest title I've ever had added to my name is *FATHER!* After a great deal of thought I said; I would tell her: When a woman's world falls apart the first thing she does is blame her man. 'Life is filled with a multitude of amazing choices. Most women don't want to accept the fact that their life is a direct result of the decisions they made. It is more feasible for them to pass the liability on to their man.

The man being at fault is the number one answer for seventy five percent of anything that goes wrong in a woman's life. The other twenty five percent is reserved for blaming her children and parents. Even when a woman doesn't have a man. It's still the man's fault. I once overheard a woman say, she had gained seventy pounds in the last year because she didn't have a man. I asked her why she didn't have a man, and of course she gave the number one cliché; *"a good man is hard to find."* If I had a dime for every time I've heard this said I'd be wealthy enough to pay for the health care of all the people in the United States. This has got to be the number one socially acceptable excuse for women who are not in a good relationship. Women tend to pick a man apart piece by piece, like he's some sort of puzzle. They'll say; *he's too weak, he's too ugly, he's too poor, he's too light, he's too dark, he's too mean, he's too religious, he's too worldly, he's too boring, he drinks too much, he eats too much, he can't dance, his teeth are crooked, he thinks he's all of that, he don't make enough money, his car is too raggedy, he lives with his momma;* then the next statement she makes after this list of all he's not is; "*that's why I don't have a man.*" Women put themselves in and out of a relationship all at the same time.

Now I'm not saying that men are perfect. Clearly, I'm not saying that. However, women need to take inventory on all she's not first, before focusing in on his lack. Maybe then she'll see him for more of what he is as opposed to what he ain't. Of course men play their part in the down fall of a relationship. However, this does not alleviate the fact that a woman has many signs before the whole thing comes crashing down. She should pay close attention to what is going on and be willing to take responsibility for her part. If she doesn't, she'll take that exact same mistake into her next relationship. Accepting responsibility for your mistakes is key to personal growth. The truth is, if you keep doing the same thing you been doing, all you're going to get is what you've already got. This is true for men and women. Therefore, this would be the first piece of advice I'd give my daughter. Don't be so quick to blame your man. Accept responsibility for the decisions you made and grow from the experience.

The second point of guidance I would

offer her is direct, hard core truth. Men are seventy five percent physical and sixty percent of that is sexual. This means, they want what they can see, hear, touch, taste, smell. They don't work off of erratic imagination like women. Men are not sitting back thinking about how beautiful his weddings going to be when he gets married. Nor is his mind consumed with the thoughts of how nurturing he's going to be to his children. His mind works just like this; sense number 1: *Sight,* he sees a woman that peaks his interest sexually. Sense number 2: *Hearing*, he listens only long enough to learn what words he needs to say to get to the next sense. Sense number 3.*Touch*, he wants to have sex with her. Numbers 4 and 5 is self explanatory, he wants to smell food cooking and eat. You have just satisfied sixty percent of his needs. There is the twenty five percent devoted to making money. Then there is fifteen percent devoted to emotions that are not directly attached to his penis and the greatest percentage of that is reserved for family. I would want my daughter to understand this does not mean a man is shallow. He is not. I'm emphatically stating a man is simple. I do not want her to over load her mind with unnecessary thoughts that will have no basis on his happiness in a relationship.

What I've learned in seventy years of life is you can spend a lifetime searching for that special someone. You go on date after date in search of the "right one", then one day you realize all the dates, all the questions, all the answers , are only a mere glimpse into what or who a person truly is. After four marriages, I can genuinely state without prejudice it is self evident that you don't know what you're getting, until you got it. This is why the most important piece of advice I can give my daughter is; love and respect yourself with the love of God. Get plenty of formal education and protect your feelings, don't just give them away. This way even If she does not get the first two pieces of advice right this third piece of advice will surely protect her from the inconsequential, weak men that are awaiting her in this world.

Like you gentlemen, I'm going to share some of my thoughts, for ladies to think about.

The way I see it there's no shortage of good men, just women who keep trying to fit a round peg into a square whole. No matter what, if the situation does not feel right in her heart and in her mind she will know, just let it go. It will be hard but she must face her challenges head on knowing that her trials and tribulations will come to strengthen her, not leave her weak and desperate. When she sees things are not what they should be, set yourself free.

Take your time to pick a mate, don't choose to loose, and don't stay until it's too late. You will only get what you go after.

Love is the only truth. Without it life is one big, empty existence.

I truly concur with my friend; simply put marriage is a state we all long to belong to. However, if you marry the wrong person you would have sentenced yourself to a relationship of stress, fury and illness.

To me marriage is an institution combined of three things; a partnership, a business arrangement and a sexual limited liability corporation.

My personal belief is there is no such thing as cheating, only self satisfaction. It is better for a person to stray outside of a relationship than to swindle yourself out of long overdue happiness. That's why I love when David said, he wishes there was a sex depository.

Try to date in equal interest. Don't give away your cookies to someone who's not really interested in them. Your common ground should be mutual interest. Take me for example; the right woman starts with enjoying good food, good wine, and great sex, non argumentative, financially independent and she must have an outstanding lust for life. For me to have a woman who lacks even one of these traits would be uncivilized. Like Charles mentioned, do not apply, if you're not qualified.

I truly enjoyed when Charles said; listen to the voice inside your heart and keep thinking positive; if you don't sadness will take you over quick, fast and in a hurry. Choose to be happy. Fill your mind with thoughts of greatness not thoughts of dread.

Love expands beyond all perception. Yet somehow we find it to be a game that's to be won. Loves is not a win or lose game, it is, however, a pursuit for the fulfillment of never ending desires. It can never be won, because the minute you get that one desire fulfilled instantly, another yearning steps in from the background and anxiously waits to be satisfied.

Cherish the times you have sex. Because every time you have sex something comes along with it. Sometimes you won't be able to see it coming. For example: a sexually transmitted disease, a baby or a fatal attraction. The least you will ever walk away with, from a sexual experience, is a memory. Make sure you protect your body and mind and only have intimacy with a person you trust and desire, mentally and physically.

Always trust your first mind. Never dispel your beliefs about what's going on and deprive yourself of the truth. Believe it or not, truth is happiness.

As Kenneth said, "Don't let anyone have your self confidence".

Like Chico said, don't be too quick to trust. Keep a quiet self. If you just listen a person will tell you everything you want to know.

Protect your heart don't give it up to easy, or you'll find yourself going in circles or even worst, backwards.

Most of all remember

LIVING IS THE PRICE
YOU PAY FOR LIFE.
SINCE YOU'RE ALREADY PAYING
YOU MAY AS WELL GET THE BEST
YOU CAN FROM IT.
KEEP IN MIND
YOU WILL ONLY GET WHAT YOU
GO AFTER!!!

I'm C. J. Big, and I want to sum it up with a plain old simple truth my Father taught me;

DO NOT TROUBLE YOUR MIND
OVER THINKING, THE BASIC NEEDS
OF AN INDIVIDUAL.
THIS IS WHAT YOU NEED TO
KNOW;

Men require the three F's
Food
Finances
&
F#@%ing

Women require the three T's
Time
Trust
&
Things

For a woman, if a man messes up on the ***trust*** *he must double up on the* ***time*** *and* ***things!!!***

For a man, if she's lacking ***finances,*** *she's got*

to be good at ***food*** *and* ***well you know!!!***

MOST OF ALL JUST, ***HUSH***
WHILE YOUR MAN IS TALKING!!!
YOU MIGHT LEARN A LOT MORE
THAN YOU CAN IMAGINE!!!

Thanks Dad!!!

www.ingramcontent.com/pod-product-compliance
Lightning Source LLC
La Vergne TN
LVHW050645100826
845148LV00011B/1994

* 9 7 8 0 9 8 1 7 5 4 4 1 3 *